The Power to Change
THE WORLD
THE WELSH AND AZUSA STREET REVIVALS

RICK JOYNER

MorningStar Publications
A DIVISION OF MORNINGSTAR FELLOWSHIP CHURCH
375 Star Light Drive, Fort Mill, SC 29715

The Power to Change the World
by Rick Joyner
Copyright © 2006
Third Printing, 2008

Distributed by MorningStar Publications, Inc.,
a division of MorningStar Fellowship Church
375 Star Light Drive, Fort Mill, SC 29715
www.MorningStarMinistries.org
1-800-542-0278.

International Standard Book Number: 978-1-929371-72-3; 1-929371-72-1

Cover Design: Kevin Lepp
Book Layout: Dana Zondory

TABLE OF CONTENTS

PART ONE

THE WELSH REVIVAL

CHAPTER ONE
THEY LOVED GOD

You are about to read two accounts of the most exciting acts of God in the last two thousand years. This is the story of the two greatest revivals in history: the Welsh Revival which began in 1904, and the Azusa Street Revival which began in 1906. These accounts are so amazing that without question if they had taken place in the first century they would have been highlights in the Book of Acts.

The accounts of these revivals are so remarkable that even many Christians today are skeptical when they hear of the things that took place. How could Wales, the little principality on the British Isles, become the center of the world's attention for nearly two years? How could a converted stable turned into a mission on Azusa Street be considered possibly the most famous address in the world? However, these events are so widely corroborated, even in secular newspapers and journals from around the world, that we must conclude this was just an extraordinary time in which the Lord wanted to show what He could do with even the most humble people who would give Him their lives.

These revivals were but a foretaste of an even greater move of God that will soon come—the one that the Lord Himself called **"the harvest,"** which will come at the end of the age (see Matthew 13:39). This is why we must understand these revivals, not just to be encouraged, but prepared. God will do it again, only bigger.

That these two extraordinary moves of God broke out so closely together in time, less than two years apart, was no coincidence. Though nearly ten thousand miles separated them, a huge distance at the time, there were bridges between them. Just as the combination of some principles, such as faith and love, releases a power far greater than what either of these have alone, the uniting of different moves of God with different emphases can multiply the power of each. That is what happened in the case of these two revivals. Likewise, the combination of these two stories together seems to be much more powerful than the telling of either one individually.

Even though these two revivals were alike in many ways, and one could even be considered an extension and completion of the other, they were also each different in some basic ways, which is important for us to understand. In both their likenesses and their differences, there are profound and significant lessons for anyone who is devoted to seeing and being a part of a true move of God.

GOD MOVED

A move of God is, by its very definition, God moving. In the very first mention of the Holy Spirit in Scripture, He is moving (see Genesis 1:2). That is His basic nature, and He will not change. Those who are led by the Spirit are also moving, going somewhere, and are always focused on a purpose and destiny.

When the Holy Spirit moves, there cannot help but to be consequences, and they are not arbitrary. The Holy Spirit is not just expending energy when He moves. Just as the first time He moved and brought forth the glorious creation of the earth, He is moving now to bring forth the glorious new creation—mankind made again in His image. Those He uses for His great purpose are being propelled into the greatest adventure, and the most exciting and fulfilling life that can be had upon the earth. To not be prepared can likewise be an ultimate tragedy. On that great judgment day there will be no greater remorse than to have not fulfilled our purpose so as to hear the greatest of all words from the King: **"Well done, good and faithful servant!" (Matthew 25:21 NIV)**

THE EARTH WILL SHAKE

The whole world was shaken by these revivals that we are going to study, and we need to understand how and why this happened. When God moves, the earth will shake just as it did when He descended upon Mount Sinai. The greater the move of God, the greater the shaking that will take place.

When the earth shakes, people become fearful, even paranoid, which can even happen to those who are sincere seekers of God. This is why, after the Lord descended on Mount Sinai, the people of Israel came to Moses and asked him to intercede for them so that they would not have to endure such fear again. There will never be anything more exciting or wonderful than being close to God. He is an awesome God. Revival is very serious business; we are not going to a spiritual amusement park, but into the presence of the greatest King.

One of the ways that we can be prepared is to understand that when God moves, the earth will shake. That the greatest move of God of all time is soon to be upon us is both the greatest hope and the most sober warning, as we are given in Hebrews 12:18-29:

> **For you have not come to a mountain that may be touched and to a blazing fire, and to darkness and gloom and whirlwind,**

> **and to the blast of a trumpet and the sound of words which sound was such that those who heard begged that no further word should be spoken to them.**

> **For they could not bear the command, "If even a beast touches the mountain, it will be stoned."**

> **And so terrible was the sight, that Moses said, "I am full of fear and trembling."**

> **But you have come to Mount Zion and to the city of the living God, the heavenly Jerusalem, and to myriads of angels,**

to the general assembly and church of the first-born who are enrolled in heaven, and to God, the Judge of all, and to the spirits of righteous men made perfect,

and to Jesus, the mediator of a new covenant, and to the sprinkled blood, which speaks better than the blood of Abel.

See to it that you do not refuse Him who is speaking. For if those did not escape when they refused him who warned them on earth, much less shall we escape who turn away from Him who warns from heaven.

And His voice shook the earth then, but now He has promised, saying, "Yet once more I will shake not only the earth, but also the heaven."

And this expression, "Yet once more," denotes the removing of those things which can be shaken, as of created things, in order that those things which cannot be shaken may remain.

Therefore, since we receive a kingdom which cannot be shaken, let us show gratitude, by which we may offer to God an acceptable service with reverence and awe;

for our God is a consuming fire.

True revival is a holy, fearful thing. However, there is good fear and bad fear, and revival is definitely good fear.

If we will embrace the true, pure, and holy fear of God, we will not have to fear anything else on this earth. The good fear, the holy fear of God, is actually the foundation of true faith. In this, we must understand that there is an enemy of every move of God, and his main weapon against us is the evil fear. There will be an increasing conflict of fear and faith in the times ahead.

Immature, inexperienced, or insecure believers often try to water down the concept of fearing God. Some modern Bible translations will even use the word "respect" in place of fear when it comes to God. However, anyone who actually encountered the Lord in the Scriptures, or history, would probably search for an even stronger word than fear to use for that encounter. Even the Apostle John, near the end of his life, having been the most intimate of the Lord's disciples, and having walked the earth as an apostle longer than anyone else, when he had the revelation and saw the Lord Jesus, he fell to the ground like a dead man. That was a little more than just respect!

The Lord is our most loving Father, who loved us so much that He even sent His only Son to make atonement for us. He is affectionate and loves His children more than any earthly father ever could—but He is still God and we must never forget this! The Apostle John was intimate with Jesus, but Judas was familiar—so familiar that he would even casually sop his bread with the King of kings. Such presumption based on mere familiarity with God will prove increasingly deadly in the times ahead. Any move of God will be both the most wonderful experience we can have, and the most serious business we could ever be involved in.

THE RIDE OF A LIFETIME

Every true move of God in history has had an impact upon the church, and to at least some degree has brought change to possibly the whole church. What is coming is going to bring some of the most radical changes that the church has ever experienced, and they will also be coming faster than ever before. Much more is going to be accomplished in the next few decades than has been accomplished in the last five centuries. Are we ready? As is usually the case, those who would cheer the most at the prospect of this will be some of the most affected, especially those who presume that God sees everything the way they do.

It is no accident that when a true revival breaks out there is often a great earthquake, and sometimes more than one. World history now gives its attention to the earthquakes during the times of these revivals, but the earthquakes were actually a result of the way the Lord was moving at that time. People today may chafe at such a notion, but these revivals were actually bigger news in the world press at the time than even the San Francisco earthquake.

Like the earthquakes, these two great revivals erupted with very little warning. They came like two tsunamis, but from different directions, catching the whole world off balance each time. These revivals profoundly impacted and changed the church worldwide as few moves of God ever have. Together they set the church on a course into the future that very few had foreseen or were prepared for.

This resulted in some of the greatest growth, spiritual advances, and conflicts in the church since the first century. The impact of these two revivals was so great that it simply is not possible to understand the modern church, or where it is headed, without understanding these revivals.

The fact that these two powerful revivals happened so closely together in time multiplied the impact of each of them. They caused the greatest transformation of church life since the Reformation, and in the opinion of some, since the first century. However, as great as this impact was, they did not birth the church into its full purpose. These were but a part of "the beginning of birth pangs" (see Matthew 24:8, I Thessalonians 5:3) as prophesied by both the Lord Jesus and Paul. There have been other great spiritual birth contractions since, and each have helped to move the church relentlessly toward what will be the greatest of the great moves of God ever to come upon the earth—the going forth of the gospel of the kingdom in kingdom power.

A VISION OF THE WAVE

Moves of God are often called "waves of the Holy Spirit" by church historians because they often behave like waves of the sea. Likewise, catching and riding a wave of the Holy Spirit can be like surfing. To surf you need to learn how to discern the pattern of waves and where they are breaking. Then you need to position yourself in the right place, and begin moving in the right direction at the right time, if you are going to catch and ride the wave. The same is required for catching the waves of the Spirit.

On May 11, 1992, I had a prophetic experience in which I saw the church like a surfer floating on a short surfboard. He was gazing at the beach, lazily drifting and dreaming of the big wave. While this surfer was drifting, the very wave he was dreaming about was getting closer and closer, but he did not know it. I knew that unless he woke up and looked around quickly, it was going to come crashing down on top of him. The result was not going to be a smooth ride, but rather a serious problem! I also knew his board was too short for the huge wave that was coming.

Because of his sleepy state, the very wave this surfer dreamed about placed him in serious jeopardy. By the time he heard the sound of the wave and turned to look, it was too late. What had been the desire of his heart became a terror. He was not awake and watching for the wave when it came, and therefore was unprepared. The wave turned the surfer over and over, smashing him into the bottom several times and breaking his board. I feared for his life, but he did survive with many cuts, bruises, and a few broken bones.

I watched the surfer lying on the beach in great pain. Soon the terror of possibly dying passed and a deep wisdom replaced it. He gazed back out over the sea. Even though he was so broken and hurt that he could hardly move, an awesome resolve and dignity came over him. I knew he would come back to ride the waves again.

I then saw this surfer in a hospital with a room that looked out over the ocean. He was still gazing out over the sea, but I knew that instead of dreaming, he was now planning. I then saw him standing on the beach, not only healed, but in far better shape than he had been before. Next to him stood the largest surfboard I have ever seen. He was going to catch the big one, and he was prepared.

Even though the sea was calm, I knew and he knew that the biggest wave of all was already in motion beyond the horizon. You could just feel it. The surfer was ready for it this time, but I also saw fear begin to rise in him. I knew that if he did not quickly dismiss it and get moving, he would not be able to paddle out far enough in time and would again miss the great wave.

Then I looked around and saw many other surfers who looked like professional bodybuilders standing all over the beach. These all had the same kind of short boards that the original surfer had at first. These bodybuilders really did not seem interested in the waves at all, but just in looking good. However, their bodies actually looked grotesque to anyone but themselves. I also knew that their large, bulging muscles were not as strong as those of the real surfer, whose muscles seemed more natural. The vision ended.

INTERPRETATION

In many ways the interpretation of this vision is obvious. In the previous great awakenings or revivals in church history, there have been very few individuals who were anticipating the move of the Holy Spirit. In almost every great awakening or revival, the existing churches and ministries were damaged by the new move because they were not ready for it. Some of these had to actually resist the revival, fighting the wave of the Spirit, just to survive.

In contrast, today there seems to be almost a universal expectation of impending revival, but very little has actually been done to prepare for it. Even though we may know it is coming, many are spending more time dreaming about it than preparing for it. The actual wave of the Holy Spirit that is coming is bigger than we have dreamed, but because we are dreaming instead of watching for it and preparing, many are now in serious jeopardy.

That the first surfboard was so short and obviously inadequate for even a good size wave, much less the awesome one that came, speaks of the inadequacy of the current vehicles, meaning outreaches and ministries of the church. I felt that even if the surfer had seen the wave in time, he could not have ridden it with that little board. He would have either had to quickly paddle onto the beach, or go out beyond where the wave was going to break to watch it go by.

Since I received this vision in 1992, much of the world has experienced the greatest move of God possibly in history to date. It has had a remarkable impact in many nations and even continents. However, I feel that many of these churches which had been longing and praying for these moves of God suffered just like the unprepared surfer in many ways. Likewise, the nets were inadequate to hold the great catch, and though the fruit has been great, much of it was unnecessarily lost.

I also believe that those parts of the world, especially Europe and North America, which did not experience the great moves of God as did the rest of the world over the last few decades, are about to experience them. Like this surfer, the present church in the West is in danger of getting nothing more than a good beating and a good lesson out of the impending move of the Holy Spirit. Even though the church has been hearing from the Lord about the coming ingathering, we have not been acting on His words and actually taking practical steps to be ready for what is coming.

Even so, this beating will immediately bring wisdom and the resolve to be ready for the next one, and to have the proper vehicle for riding it. The time we spend recovering from the injuries of the impending wave must be spent in planning for the next one; then, our plans must be turned into actions.

To ride the wave that is coming, we will also need to be much stronger than we are now. Strength comes from *exercising*. When the surfer returned to the beach, he had the physique of a bodybuilder, but one who had built himself up for strength and not just show. Every muscle was perfectly formed and powerful.

The body of Christ must likewise be built up, but for strength and not just show. Every muscle and every limb, or every individual part of the body, must be properly exercised and brought to full strength. For decades we have been preaching on Ephesians 4, concerning the equipping of the saints for the work of service, but it is now time that we start doing it.

The Ephesians 4 emphasis of equipping the saints will again become fashionable. We can expect many to become involved in this "spiritual bodybuilding" just for show. These will in truth be devoted more to impressing each other than to preparing for the next move of the Spirit. They will not really have the proper equipment for, or even be aware of, what is going on in the sea. We must get our attention off of how we look to each other and on how we appear before God.

APPLICATION

Those who build their congregations for show will actually look grotesque and will not have the proper skills for riding the wave of the Spirit. Most won't even be in the water or in the proper place when the wave comes, because they are so much more interested in impressing each other.

Even though the surfer, who had been so injured by the first wave, was properly prepared and had a proper board for riding the next wave, the enemy used the negative experience of the previous wave to hit him with a fear that could hinder him from accomplishing all he had prepared for. All of our preparation and work will come to nothing if we are not utterly committed to getting back in the water and walking by faith, not by fear. To catch the wave we must:

1. Be adequately trained and in shape.
2. Have the proper board (vehicle or ministry).
3. Be properly positioned (having discerned where the wave is going to break and getting there).

4. Be watching so that we can, at the proper time, start moving in the right direction with the wave.

5. Be ready to act without hesitation when the wave breaks—get up on the board and ride it.

Even though the church worldwide has experienced remarkable awakenings, revivals, and great harvests of souls over the last few decades, the greatest is still yet to come. We do need to learn the lessons from these. However, it is important that we look forward more than looking back. For this reason I will even be tying these stories of the great Welsh and Azusa Street Revivals into a prophetic vision of the future.

As we see in Matthew 13:30, the harvest begins with the tares. Many of the revelations of wrongdoing and sin within the church have actually been a work of the Holy Spirit to prepare the church for the ingathering, which is soon to begin. There are still many tares and even stumbling blocks in the church which must be rooted out before the great and final harvest of the age begins.

Every time the Lord has shown me the coming harvest, He has shown it to me in two great waves. There may be more than two waves coming, but I know there will be at least two. As I have often said, the first wave will be so great that almost everyone will believe it is in fact the great harvest that is at the end of the age. However, there is at least one more wave coming after it that will be much greater. The millions of new believers that will, or possibly have already come on the first wave, are all called to be laborers in the second one. These people must be properly equipped and prepared for the greater wave.

We must fulfill the Ephesians 4 mandate to equip the saints to do the work of the ministry. The present structure of the typical local church, which is more like a spectator sport than its biblical counterpart, with a few people doing everything and the rest just cheering, will not survive much longer. The waves of the Spirit that are coming will either badly damage or destroy those who have not fulfilled this basic mandate of true New Testament ministry. The first wave of revival that is coming on the church will be a blessing only to the churches that have been using their time wisely and have been truly equipping the saints to do the work of the service. This wave will actually be judgment on every ministry which has not been properly equipping its people, or has spent more time dreaming than preparing.

Just as surfing is not the safest of sports, placing one in the domain of the most fearsome of predators (sharks), riding the waves of revival is not for the timid, just as true Christianity is not for the timid. Those who are ruled more by fear than by faith will soon be found out, and they will not be a part of what will be the greatest move of God upon the earth.

Like sharks, the devil and his minions will swarm toward a move of God to try to pick off any one they can in an effort to chase the rest away too. Why would the Lord allow such a thing? Because true spiritual advances can never go far if there are many fearful and timid people around. It takes the greatest faith and courage to be a part of true revival. For those who are led by the Spirit, who walk by faith rather than fear, to experience even a short ride with the Holy Spirit is worth risking everything. Those who are not willing to risk are not worthy of revival.

WHAT IS REVIVAL?

I have good friends who do not like the word "revival," but I think it is appropriate for describing every move of God since the first century. What we call a new move of God is almost always a restoration of what has been lost by the church since the first century. Each revival is a reviving of something that, if not dead and needing a resurrection, was at least asleep. But what is it that we are after?

The Lord is always with us and will be when even two are gathered together. Even so, there is a great difference between this and the "manifest presence of the Lord." The life of Moses is a good example of how the manifest presence of the Lord can change us. He was eighty years old, having spent the last forty years of his life in the lowest profession of the times, as a shepherd. He was probably considered by all, including himself, as washed up and finished! However, one encounter with the manifest presence of the Lord changed this washed up old man into a spiritual giant who delivered a nation.

Throughout the Scriptures, we see these encounters with God that transform as nothing else can. Both the Welsh and Azusa Street Revivals were encounters that transformed and released some of the greatest men and women of God on the earth, possibly since the Book of Acts was written. Throughout church history, we find that even the slightest breakthrough of the presence of the Lord not only sparked revivals and brought transformation to the church, but also sent shock waves throughout society. The greater the manifestation of His presence, the greater the revivals. The more profound the transformations, the more powerful the shock waves.

Some church historians trace the transformations of the church more to the illumination of certain biblical truths that were lost or overlooked. There is some merit to this perspective. It is the truth that sets us free. However, the Truth is a Person. It is not the encounter with an idea as much as it is the encounter with God that we need for true, heart transformation. Facts can change minds, but the manifest presence of the Lord changes hearts and minds. It is only when we have this ultimate revelation that we are seeking the Person of Truth, Jesus Christ, that true revival comes.

Even so, we cannot love the Truth Himself without loving all truth, especially the truth of the Scriptures and sound doctrine. As we discussed above, a combination of such things as truth and love can multiply the power of each. When the prophets and teachers learn to worship together like they did at Antioch, the Lord will release true apostolic authority in the earth again.

As the Lord warned in Matthew 22:29, we will go into error because we do not know the Scriptures and the power of God. Some who know the Scriptures will go into error because they do not know His power, and those who know His power tend to go into error because they do not know the Scriptures as they should. We need both together, and the harvest that is the end of the age, the greatest of all moves of God, will be a result of a marriage between these two.

However, if we love the Scriptures without loving Him more, they can even become an idol that eclipses our love for God. If we love the power of God more than we love Him, we will likewise fall into an idolatry of the power. Again, we need both together in proper balance. Even so, one moment in the manifest presence of the Lord can transform a person more than many years of teaching and preaching. This is not to negate the need for teaching and preaching, which are themselves some of the greatest gifts from God to us, but these are only the scaffolding of the building—the building is the Lord Himself. We are seeking to grow up into Him.

What good is the most glorious temple if God is not in it? If God is in it, no one will be focused on the temple, regardless of how glorious it is—their attention will be on the God who inhabits it. This is what true revivalists have always been in pursuit of: the Lord Himself and His manifest presence. Once we have experienced His manifest presence, we are forever ruined for anything else. The truth of the Scriptures and the greatest miracles are wonderful, but they are far less full of wonder than the Lord Himself.

When we encounter Him, it will inevitably result in a greater love for the Scriptures, a greater love for His church, and the fellowship of others in pursuit of Him. But none of these alone can fully satisfy us—we must have Him.

This story of these two revivals is about those who sought God and found Him. The encounter with Him that they experienced sent spiritual tidal waves and tsunamis around the world. Like tsunamis, when God moves this way, everything that is not on high enough ground will be in danger of destruction. Churches and movements that have fallen from their high calling will be washed away. The glories of these revivals astonished the world, but they also brought a judgment to those who were not rightly positioned when they came. This history will repeat itself—both the glory and the judgment. We must understand that this is not just history, but prophecy.

I have written about each of these revivals in my books, *The World Aflame* and *The Fire That Would Not Die*. Though these books were very successful, they have not been as widely distributed as many of my other works. However, for those who have read them, they seem inevitably to become their favorites, as they are mine. This work is a combination of these two books, along with additional material and insights that I have acquired in the years since they were written. I have done this because, as I stated above, combining these two stories does seem to multiply the power of each.

These stories include some of the most exciting testimonies of God's works in this age. They are also filled with very important principles, methods, and insights into God's ways, but the most important of all is that God is yearning to be sought after. Anyone who seeks Him will find Him, and those who find Him cannot help but to love Him. The love of God is not only our greatest treasure; it is the most powerful force that will ever impact the earth. Believing God can move mountains, but loving God can move nations. This is my main prayer for all who read this book—that your love for God will increase so that you will become contagious with an authentic, genuine passion for Him.

To experience revival, one must love the approval of God more than men. The degree to which we are concerned about what other people think of us will inhibit the degree to which we can be used while on the earth. We must have a higher goal of being concerned with the way heaven sees us, not those on the earth whose vision will be distorted. The greatest testimony that we can have in heaven is to be known as one who loves God. This is our highest calling. This is the main thing, and He is worthy to be loved. When we set our hearts on loving Him revival will come.

I have studied church history for over thirty-five years. Much of that has been devoted especially to revivals or unique and powerful moves of God such as the great Reformation movements. The two we are going to study here are to me by far the most interesting and compelling. Even so, I do not consider myself a historian, but rather a student of history. Neither do I consider myself an expert on these revivals, but I am sharing with you some of the great treasures I found in my study of them, which I think can also be of great practical help in preparing us for what is to come.

Looking back at history is much like looking ahead prophetically. We see in part and we know in part; so if we want the complete picture, we will have to put what we have together with what others have. Therefore, I have tried to compile many of the different accounts, but in doing this, I did at times find conflicts between them. In these cases, I have tried to weigh the evidence and choose the account that I thought was the most accurate. At times, I have included both seemingly conflicting accounts, because I felt there was probably some truth to both. However, my real goal is not just to share insights from history, but to help prepare those who will make history.

CHAPTER TWO
ORIGINS

The first known spark of the work of God that became the Welsh Revival actually took place in Scranton, Pennsylvania. A Welsh pastor with a thriving church was thrilling his audiences with his oratory and intellect. Then suddenly he became broken before God and saw that he was not a true prophet of the New Testament type. As he was filled with remorse over his true state, he had a glorious experience of the fullness of the Spirit. At once his preaching changed—eloquence had been replaced by passion. He also became burdened for his beloved Wales and resigned from his church in Scranton to return to his homeland.

To the consternation of the religious people in Wales who knew him before he left for America, the young minister returned filled with a strange sense of urgency. No longer did he preach for effect—to stir the congregation to great emotional heights. He preached for results—the salvation of souls and the awakening of the

Lord's people. "It was," as one observer said, "indeed a strange thing to see Welsh Preaching-festivals converted into what approximated very nearly to Holiness Conventions when he was there! All believed in the sincerity of the preacher, but most could not understand him, and many became hostile."

This began in 1879. Even though this young preacher was being maligned and persecuted, he stayed on course and soon began deeply affecting the other young ministers of his own denomination. The passion for the presence of God in these young men bound them into a holy fellowship that was to last for years to come. In the providence of God, early in 1903, these men found themselves occupying pulpits near each other so that their fellowship could continue.

Their intensified desperation to have all that God had for them soon turned into a consciousness of the presence of God in their midst. These pastors began to note that after a period of agonizing intercession, there would be unusual power for the preaching of the Word the following day. Glorious experiences beget more faith, and soon this little group of young ministers was convinced that something glorious was going to happen in their midst.

Dr. F.B. Meyer had been used in a wonderful way to minister to fellow preachers in South Wales, so this fellowship of the zealous wrote to him and invited him to come and minister to them concerning the deep things of God. He replied that there would be a "Keswick Convention" at the beautiful Welsh spa of Llandridod

Wells that year, and invited them to attend, which they did. God moved on these young men mightily, and they all came into an even deeper knowledge of the holy things of God.

Looking back, many considered this convention to be a major step up the mountain to the great transfiguration that was coming. There were other steps, too. Those who have been a part of great awakenings or revivals could almost all look back and see a remarkable, carefully planned course they had unknowingly followed.

In August 1904, a second convention at Llandridod Wells took place. Dr. F.B. Meyer and Dr. A.T. Pierson ministered. Again the power and glory of God was present to transform. The Welsh saints were so overcome with the glory of God that they sang over and over the great chorus: "CROWN HIM LORD OF ALL!"

Meanwhile in Cardinganshire, in a tiny village named New Quay, the Lord had been quietly preparing other instruments for the coming awakening. The Rev. Joseph Jenkins had been deeply concerned about the lack of anointing in his own preaching, which compelled him to desperately seek a deeper life in Christ. Andrew Murray's book, *With Christ in the School of Prayer,* came into his possession and moved him greatly at this time. He became increasingly burdened by the indifference among the Christians around him and the apathy of the young people in his own church. He exhorted them earnestly about obeying the Spirit. This was in the early part of the year 1904.

A TESTIMONY LIGHTS THE FIRE

The kindling was now ready, but the spark to light the fire would come from an even more unlikely source. In a Sunday morning prayer meeting for young people, Pastor Jenkins asked for testimonies of spiritual experiences. Several tried to speak on other subjects, but the pastor stopped them. At last a young girl named Florrie Evans, who had been gloriously converted just a few days before, stood and with a trembling voice said: "I LOVE JESUS CHRIST WITH ALL MY HEART!"

With these simple words, the sparks that God had planted in so many hearts burst into open flame. Many consider this to be the true beginning of the great Welsh Revival. The fire quickly spread to Blaenanerch, Newcastle Emlyn, Capel Drindod, and Tregwynt. Streams spread abroad like lava from a great volcano—soon multiplied thousands were aflame with the Holy Spirit's testimony of the glorious Son of God.

As the blessing in New Quay was quickly noised abroad, doors began to open on every hand. Led by their pastor, this group of young people, most of whom were between sixteen and eighteen years of age, conducted meetings throughout the south of the country. The fire continued to increase and leap over every boundary that tried to contain it. Conventions and conferences sprang up all over Wales, emphasizing holiness of heart and life in the Spirit. The Lord mightily used such men as W.S. Jones, E. Keri Evans, Jake Thickens, Seth and Frank Joshua, John Pugh, and R.B. Jones.

In August 1904, in the city of Cardiff, the famous evangelist R.A. Torrey held a service that resulted in many salvations. From every direction the Lord seemed to be bringing more fuel for the flames now growing in Wales. In November of the same year, in Rhos, North Wales, the churches invited the esteemed preacher, R.B. Jones to conduct a campaign. He had entered into the Spirit-filled life the previous year and his entire ministry changed. He burned with a new message, and news about him which was spreading throughout Britain. In God's proper timing, this flaming evangelist added to the growing fire in Wales.

In Rhos, the professing Christians broke down before God and began to remove the hindrances in their lives. They committed themselves to full surrender to Christ and the reception of the Spirit in His fullness. The floodgates of heaven opened and the Spirit was poured out in torrents. The numbers grew until the churches overflowed nightly. Four weeks after Jones left Rhos, a Wrexham paper reported that "the whole district is in the grip of an extraordinary spiritual force which shows no sign of relaxing its hold."

Already the meetings were being carried on by the people themselves, regardless of whether pastors were present or not. The meetings started in the morning and continued through the evenings and into the night. Then they began to spill over into the streets, into the homes, the trains, the factories, and the mines. Soon great processions of awakened Christians and new converts were marching through towns singing hymns and rejoicing in the Savior.

By this time there were approximately forty thousand believers who had been radically touched by God and were desperate for God to pour out His Spirit in Wales. Most of these were in groups that were yet unknown to each other and were scattered throughout the land. When the Spirit began to link them together, in order to release one of the great demonstrations of the mighty power of God in answer to their prayers, not only would the entire principality of Wales soon be aflame with the fire of God, but much of the world would soon be ablaze.

CHAPTER THREE

FUEL FOR THE FIRE

It was in late 1904 that the revival which many consider to be the greatest in history broke out in Wales. There have been a few spiritual awakenings in history to span the globe and touch millions, but it can be argued that none had as much concentrated impact as the Welsh Revival in its time. It seems that the Lord looked down upon Wales and said, "I am going to show the church and the world what I can do with just a handful of faithful saints who will yield themselves to Me." The results of that demonstration still send shock waves of conviction and hope to all who hear the story.

LIGHT SHINES IN THE DARKNESS

At the time, the overall spiritual condition of Wales was as dark as it had ever been. Bars flourished. Football (soccer), cockfighting, prize fighting, gambling, and prostitution seemed to have completely captured the soul of the working class. Murder, rape, and other violent crimes were common and increasing at a dramatic rate. It seemed that the authorities were close to losing what control they had.

The dark tunnels of the Welsh coal mines seemed a fitting symbol of what was happening to the country. However, from among those miners God was preparing a voice. He emerged from the mines to preach the Gospel just as Wales began to emerge from the dark pits of her sin. Soon this young miner, Evan Roberts and tiny little Wales would cause the whole world to pause and take notice of the wonderful works of God.

Evan Roberts was born on June 8, 1878, in a working-man's cottage called "Island House." It was a modest home with eight small rooms. No one then could have suspected that for decades to come, pilgrims would travel from around the world to gaze at this little house and to pray for the heavens to be opened again, as they were for Evan.

Evan began work in the mines when he was just nine years old. His father, Henry, broke his leg in the pit, so his son had to help him in his job. After a few months, Evan himself took up the work of a door-boy. It was his job to look after the doors around the pit. He was paid seventy-five cents a week. Later, he learned the trade of a blacksmith.

As Evan grew, he began to feel a burning passion to preach, but few with other ambitions ever left the mines, even those who wanted to be preachers. Once trapped in the miner's life, it was very hard to escape.

However, Evan's pastor and friends encouraged him even though his lack of education made his prospects look even more dim. Evan persevered with his vision, and when he turned twenty-six years old, he entered the preparatory school at Newcastle Emlyn. This was to prepare himself for the Trevecca College entrance examination. Evan had determined to do all that he could and to trust God to do the rest. Evan would never finish school, but many schools would one day devote their attention to studying Evan and the extraordinary move of God that he was used to spark and help lead. The Lord did not need Evan's knowledge—He only needed Evan.

For a period of time, Evan had been seeking and finding a more intimate relationship with the Lord. William Davies, a deacon at the Moriah Chapel, had counseled young Evan never to miss the prayer meetings in case the Holy Spirit would come and he would be missing. So, Evan faithfully attended the Monday evening meeting at Moriah, Tuesday at Pisgah, Wednesday at Moriah, and Thursday and Friday at other prayer meetings and Bible classes. For thirteen years he did this, faithfully praying for a mighty visitation of the Holy Spirit.

THE REVELATION

One day before school, in the spring of 1904, Evan found himself in what he later referred to as a Mount of Transfiguration experience. The Lord revealed Himself in such an amazing and overwhelming way that Evan was filled with divine awe. After this he would go through periods of uncontrollable trembling that were so pronounced, his family became concerned. For weeks, God visited Evan each night. When his family pressed him to tell about the experiences, he would only say it was something indescribable. When the time came near for him to enter grammar school at Newcastle Emlyn, he was reluctant to go, afraid that he would miss these encounters with the Lord.

At this time, the convention was being held at Blaenanerch, a few miles from his school. An evangelist named Seth Joshua was leading the meetings. On Thursday morning, September 29, 1904, Evan Roberts and nineteen other young people, including his friend Sydney Evans, attended the meeting. On the way, the Lord moved on the small company and they began to sing: "It is coming, it is coming—the power of the Holy Ghost—I receive it—I receive it—the power of the Holy Ghost."

During the seven o'clock meeting, Evan was so deeply moved that he broke down completely at the close of the service. That is when Seth Joshua first used the words that would become known as the cry of the revival, "BEND US, OH LORD!" Evan entered such travail that he heard nothing more. He later testified that the Spirit of God whispered to him: "This is what you need," which to Evan simply meant to yield to the Spirit.

"Bend me, Oh Lord," he cried over and over, but the fire did not fall. At the nine o'clock meeting, the spirit of intercession was moving on the congregation in great power. Evan was bursting to pray; then he felt the Spirit of God prompting him to do so publicly. With tears streaming down his face Evan just began to cry: "BEND ME! BEND ME! BEND ME! BEND US." Then the Holy Spirit came upon him with a mighty baptism that filled Evan with what he called "Calvary's love, and a love for Calvary." That night the message of the cross was so branded upon Evan's heart that there would be no other theme of the great revival he would soon help lead. From that night on Evan Roberts could focus on one thought—the salvation of souls at the foot of Jesus' cross. Historians would refer to that night as "Blaenanerch's great meeting."

One midnight shortly after this, Evan's roommate and closest friend, Sydney Evans, came into the room to find Evan's face shining with a holy light. Astonished, he asked what had happened. Evan replied that he had just seen the whole of Wales being lifted up to heaven in a vision. He then prophesied: "We are going to see the mightiest revival that Wales has ever known—and the Holy Spirit is coming just now. We must get ready. We must have a little band and go all over the country preaching." Suddenly he stopped and with piercing eyes he cried: "DO YOU BELIEVE THAT GOD CAN GIVE US 100,000 SOULS, NOW?"

The presence of the Lord so gripped Sydney that he could not help but believe. Later, while sitting in a chapel, Evan saw in a vision some of his old companions who were with many other young people. A voice spoke to him saying: "GO TO THESE PEOPLE." He said, "Lord, if it is Thy will, I will go." Then the whole chapel became filled with light so dazzling that he could only faintly see the minister in the pulpit. He was deeply disturbed and wanted to make sure that this vision was from the Lord. He consulted with his tutor who encouraged him to go.

THEY OBEYED

On October 31, Evan returned to his home by train having little knowledge of the great work of preparation that the Holy Spirit had already accomplished before him. His mother met him at the door and exclaimed in great surprise, "Where have you been? Why are you not at school? Are you ill?"

"No", he replied.

"Then why have you come back home?"

"Oh Mother, the Spirit has sent me back here to work among our own young people at the chapel at Moriah." Then turning to Dan, his younger brother, he said, "You shall see that there will be a great change at Loughor in less than a fortnight (two weeks). We are going to have the greatest revival that Wales has ever seen."

Evan then went straight to his pastor and asked permission to hold services for young people. On that night, after the adult prayer meeting, he asked the young people to stay behind as he wanted to speak to them. Sixteen adults and only one little girl stayed. After swallowing his initial disappointment that so few were interested, Evan began to explain in a quiet voice his reason for coming home. He said that he was simply obeying the Holy Spirit, and here at Moriah large numbers of young people were going to be saved. And above all, a mighty revival was coming to Wales!

This is how the most important meetings in the history of Wales began. It was stated that there was a cold spirit there that night, and unbelief was so thick it seemed to hang in the air. The results were so disappointing that Evan was even tempted to think his visions were some strange delusion. Would the young preacher believe the visions or the voices that were now telling him he had been duped by illusions of grandeur? It is at this point that many stray from the course that leads to the fulfill-ment of their calling. Evan would not.

He determined that he would rather be the greatest fool in Wales than miss a possible opportunity to see revival. Evan chose to stand by the vision just as he had prophesied, and the prophecy came true. Within two weeks, Loughor was changed and the first of one hundred thousand young people began streaming to the Lord. Because Evan did not despise the day of small beginnings, he was used to start one of the greatest moves of God of all time.

Chapter Four

THE COURSE IS SET

After the disappointing first service with the young people, the next day's services were held at Pisgah, a small chapel nearby that was a mission of Moriah. This was a Tuesday night and strangely the audience had significantly increased. Evan spoke on the importance of being filled with the Spirit. This meeting lasted until 10 P.M.

THE FOUR TENETS

The next day, on November 2, Evan was back at Moriah and he spoke on *The Four Great Tenets*. This was to become the foundational message of the revival, and they later became known as "The Four Points." These were the four essential conditions that Evan believed were required before revival could come. They were:

1. All sin must be confessed to God and repented of. The church has to be cleansed—the Lord's bride will be without spot, so there will be no

room for compromise with sin. If there is anything in our lives, in which there is any doubt as to whether it is good or evil—then cast it off!

2. There must be no cloud caused by unforgiveness between the believer and God. Have you forgiven *everybody*? If not, don't expect forgiveness for your own sins. The Scripture is clear—we cannot be forgiven until we have forgiven. Unforgiveness separates us from God like sin.

3. We must obey the Holy Spirit. Do what the Spirit prompts you to do. Prompt, implicit, and unquestioning obedience to the Spirit is required if we are going to be used by Him.

4. There must be public confessions of Christ as Savior. This is not just a one-time incident after our salvation experience or baptism—for the Christian it is a way of life. (Evan also believed there was a difference between confession and profession).

It was unknown to Evan when he first preached them, but these "Four Tenets" set the direction and course for the revival and helped to keep it on course for its duration. They established a foundation of repentance and then built upon a personal, living relationship with the Lord. The driving force behind the revival was not a doctrine or a human personality, but the Holy Spirit, who had come to convict the world of sin and then to lead the world to the Forgiver of sins, Jesus Christ. The Holy Spirit remained and moved powerfully for as long as He was able to do this work in simplicity, which is required for it.

On November 3, Evan met again at Moriah and taught the children to pray "Send the Holy Spirit to Moriah for Jesus' sake." He spoke that evening on "Ask, and it shall be given you." "These things must be believed," he said. "If the work is to succeed, we must believe that God is willing and able to answer our prayers. We must believe in a conquering Christ who is able to defeat all opposition." Evan was compelled to press the point with more boldness than he had ever felt before.

Now the vision was becoming more real to Evan than anything his natural eyes could yet see. He felt the power of the creative Word of God that could say: "Let there be light," when there was none. Evan was strangely confident that just by speaking it, it would happen. He did not understand all about prophecy, but that was not necessary. One does not have to understand everything about electricity before turning on the switch. Evan was going to keep prophesying until the light came.

On the next evening, after speaking for awhile, Evan threw the meeting open for prayer and testimony. The presence of the Lord was there, and the meeting lasted until midnight. It was announced that the next meeting would be for young people, but that evening just as many adults crowded into the chapel. There was a strange expectation in the air that God was going to do something marvelous and no one could bear to stay away.

When God is not moving, meetings are a burden. As C.S. Lewis once remarked, hell could be a perpetual church meeting without God. However, just as we see in the Book of Acts, when God is moving, all the people want to do is meet together, and there is nothing more interesting and compelling than anointed meetings of God's people.

It was because of a growing presence of the Lord that the youth meetings were now being attended by just as many adults. Everyone wanted in. Many of the children began to have wonderful conversions, astonishing their elders. Evan spoke from Ephesians 5:18 on not being drunk with wine but being filled with the Holy Spirit. Again the meeting lasted past midnight.

In less than a week, the meetings had gone from being cold and powerless to a level of intense anointing that neither the young preacher nor the people had witnessed before. Just days before, it had seemed that Evan's words had fallen to the floor. Now his words had the power to penetrate even the hardest heart, and genuine repentance was rolling over the people like waves. Evan's vision was being fulfilled before his eyes.

On Sunday, November 6, a visiting clergyman from another town occupied the morning pulpit. Evan sat and listened to the message. The pastor, wanting to give Evan an opportunity to obey God in what he had seen, announced that Evan would preach in the evening. Evan's subject was "The Importance of Obedience."

In his message, Evan personalized the Holy Spirit and gave the meeting into His hands. The Holy Spirit came and sixty young people responded to salvation. Evan then exhorted the people to pray: "Send the Spirit now for Christ's sake!" This meeting also lasted well past midnight, and news of it spread throughout the whole of

Loughor. The spirit of the people had gone from unbelief to hope, to expectation, and then to awe. It seemed that each night an unseen hand was turning up a spiritual thermostat a few more degrees. The prophecy was fast becoming history.

THE TEST

The Monday evening prayer meetings would never be considered one of the highlights of the Moriah Chapel services. Like most congregational prayer meetings, there were a handful of regular attendees and a few who might occasionally drop in. On Monday, November 7, the chapel was packed all the way back to the door. This had never happened before in the history of the chapel. At eight o'clock Evan Roberts arrived, opened his Bible, and read from the last chapter of Malachi:

> **But unto you that fear my name shall the Sun of righteousness arise with healing in his wings;**
>
> **And ye shall tread down the wicked; for they shall be as ashes under the soles of your feet in the day that I shall do this, saith the Lord of hosts (Malachi 4:2-3 KJV).**

Evan then astonished those in attendance by boldly declaring that this Scripture was going to be fulfilled immediately in Wales!

When the Lord first read from the prophecy in Isaiah, in His own synagogue at Nazareth, those who heard Him were likewise astonished at His boldness. The Lord spoke with an authority that required all who heard to either believe Him or reject Him. They chose to reject Him. Those who heard Evan Roberts that night in Moriah were challenged in the same way by his boldness. Those present felt that this was to be a demarcation point, and the revival would either go to the next level or fade away.

For a few brief moments, this great move of God hung in the balance. Here was the young man they had known from childhood and had worked with in the mines; and now he was declaring the Word of God with a boldness which they had never witnessed before. Evan had spoken in such a way that they were either going to have to believe God for a marvelous and unprecedented revival or reject the messenger. They chose to believe. They passed the great test. Now the spiritual atmosphere in Wales had reached its critical mass. Revival, to at least some degree, was inevitable.

THEY RECEIVED HIS MESSENGERS

Before continuing with the story of the revival, we need to address in some depth one of the most important factors that can determine whether we will experience and be used in an authentic revival. First, let us address a question that leads to this—could it be possible that this entire revival depended on the reception of this one man, Evan Roberts?

Yes! If we believe both the biblical and historic precedents of revival, it is likely that the great Welsh Revival depended on the reception of the messenger the Lord had chosen to strike the match and start the fire of revival. It is also likely that many moves of the Spirit which God intended, never happened, because His chosen vessels were rejected. This is an important biblical and historic truth. It is a critical test.

One of the greatest biblical revivals took place in the wicked, heathen city of Nineveh because its inhabitants chose to believe the most unlikely, wayward, Hebrew prophet—Jonah. Our reception of the grace of God is often dependent upon our ability to let Him use the foolish to confound the wise, the weak to confound the strong. The Lord Jesus Himself, before His departure from this realm, declared that: "**...from now on you shall not see Me until you say, *'Blessed is He who comes in the name of the Lord!'*"** (**Matthew 23:39**) By this, He was declaring that from that time on, we would not see Him unless we blessed those that He sent to us.

The Welsh Revival is one of the classic examples of how a people heard the Lord when He knocked on their door, and how they opened to Him and were able to maintain His manifest presence for a period of time. Many revivals have begun only to be quickly short-circuited by ambitious men who tried to use them for their own purposes. Many others never got started because men rejected the messengers the Lord sent to them for various reasons. The Lord is working through those who make up His body. If we reject them, we are rejecting Him. If we do this, He will go to where He will be received.

It is right that we desire to see God receive the glory, but this does not mean that men should not get any attention or recognition. One of the great ironies of church history is that those who are the most zealous for seeing that men do not steal God's glory almost never experience a true move of God. This is obviously because they reject the messengers He sends to them, usually claiming not to want to give God's glory to men. This is why the Apostle Paul was bold to defend his recognition as an apostle, because he could not rightly minister to the churches unless they recognized the purpose for which he had come to them.

We must receive a prophet *in the name of a prophet* if we are going to receive a prophet's reward (see Matthew 10:41). If we receive a prophet as just a teacher or a brother, we will miss what God could have given to us. The same is true of every ministry. We must receive a pastor as a pastor if we are going to receive the reward of his ministry. The same is true of an evangelist, teacher, or apostle. We must recognize the gift of God in the messenger to receive the gift that God is sending to us.

As we have discussed, **"God resists the proud, but gives grace to the humble" (James 4:6 NKJV), and it** takes humility to receive the message of God from another person. It is pride to only receive God's message from what we consider to be an appropriate messenger. God is looking for this humility so He can trust us with His grace. The greater the humility, the greater the grace. Nineveh showed extraordinary humility in receiving Jonah and his message, and thereby received extraordinary grace. First century Israel showed extraordinary spiritual pride by rejecting the very One who had created them, and thereby received the destruction that Nineveh had avoided.

Seeking humility is a basic and necessary quest. But those who try to be the police of the body of Christ in order to see that others are not exalting themselves have a terrible form of spiritual pride. Rejecting those He has sent to us as His provision often causes us to miss the grace of God. The Apostle Paul commended the Galatians for receiving him **"as an angel of God" (see Galatians 4:14),** even though his flesh was a trial to them.

The people of Wales demonstrated an unprecedented humility by receiving one who had grown up right in their midst as a prophet from God. The result of this humility was a commensurate outpouring of God's grace, a grace so great that it caused the whole world to marvel.

There is a delicate balance between wrongly exalting men and receiving them properly. As the Lord said, **"Truly I say to you, to the extent that you did it to one of these brothers of Mine, even the least of them, you did it to Me" (Matthew 25:40).** When men receive the ambassador of a nation with honor, they are honoring that nation. To not receive him with the proper protocol is to dishonor that nation. How much more should we receive the Lord's ambassadors with honor? There is a difference between properly honoring someone and worshiping him.

The Lord honors men and He exalts them. In fact, He promised to exalt them: **"...for everyone who exalts himself shall be humbled, but he who humbles himself *shall be exalted*" (Luke 18:14).** James said, **"Humble yourselves in the presence of the Lord, *and He will exalt you*" (James 4:10).** It is our job to humble ourselves and God's job to do the exalting. He is quite clear that if we try to do His job, He will do our job.

However, where does it say that we are to humble our neighbors? Our pastors? Our government leaders? That is one of the most basic forms of pride. To find the correct balance between properly honoring the messengers that God sends to us, without worshiping them, is indeed a crucial issue.

In Wales, for a short period of time, the church seemed to find this balance between receiving the messengers as servants of God, and yet not being overly dependent on them. The people not only honored the primary evangelists, they honored even the most humble saints whom the Lord had chosen to use. During the time of this revival, they were quick to recognize and receive the gift of God, regardless of the messenger.

Likewise, the primary evangelists were so committed to humbling themselves that both the Lord and the people were able to honor them properly. They used the attention that they were given to direct the people to the Lord. Men who are truly used by the Holy Spirit are not looking for honor or attention, but it will come, and they must have the grace to handle it properly when it does.

These were some of the foundational principles that seemed to enable God to mark Wales for its extraordinary revival. There are others that we will examine as we proceed, but these were the basic ones that made the Welsh such good soil for the coming seed. They would bear much fruit with it.

CHAPTER FIVE

THE FIRE COMES

Almost everyone in attendance at the meeting on Monday night, November 7, was moved to tears. Many cried in agony. By midnight the presence of the Lord was so intense that it could hardly be contained. The people had never experienced such deep repentance or such deep joy. Those crying in remorse for their sins could not be distinguished from those crying in ecstasy at the nearness of God. It was after 3 A.M. before an attempt to close the meeting was possible.

The next evening the people crowded into the chapel early just to be able to get seats. Everyone was talking about another great awakening, maybe even another Pentecost! But that night the meeting was cold and lifeless. Evan and a few faithful remained until almost 3 A.M., agonizing in prayer. Why had the Lord departed so quickly? Near 6 A.M., Evan and Dan finally left to go home and sleep.

Upon arriving home, they were jolted by cries of "I'm dying! I'm dying!" coming from their mother. Discouraged, she had left the meeting early the night before. Now she was crying out in agony declaring that she felt the entire weight of Calvary on her soul. Evan quickly recognized her burden and began to pray with her.

Later, Evan's mother explained that after leaving the meeting the night before she began to feel the agony of the Lord as He had endured the cold hardness of Gethsemane, which even His own disciples would not bear with Him. She felt that her leaving the chapel at such a critical time to go home and sleep had been the same rejection of an opportunity to stand with the Lord. She was devastated. Evan was wise. He did not try to comfort her—he tried to help her repent.

The Holy Spirit was working on the others in the community in the same way. The Lord had in fact been at the meeting, but had come in a form that they did not recognize. The Lord does not always come to excite us— at times He comes in silence, and demands silence to do a deeper surgery on our hearts. Sometimes He does not want to speak to us as much as He wants us to learn to just wait. The people of Loughor got the message quickly. Now it was time for Evan to be astonished at the people.

Just as Evan and his brother were trying to fall asleep, they were awakened by a strange noise in the streets. It was just 6 A.M., but the streets were noisy with crowds on their way to the early morning prayer services! The entire population of the town had responded in repentance, just as Evan's mother had. Now they were being transformed into a praying multitude who would not fall asleep in the presence of the Lord again for a very long time. No one had ever heard of anything like they saw that morning. They would see much more.

On November 9 and 10, Evan Roberts preached at the Brynteg Congregational Chapel. By the second night the entire congregation was, in the words of James Stewart, "completely carried away by spiritual emotion."

On this day, the first public reference to the Welsh Revival was made in a secular newspaper. Soon the entire press in Wales was devoted almost exclusively to covering the unprecedented revival. It would not be long before almost every major newspaper in the world picked up the story, as what was taking place in Wales would become front-page news in almost every great city of the world. The following is the short article that appeared in *The Western Mail* of Cardiff, Wales, on November 10.

GREAT CROWDS OF PEOPLE DRAWN TO LOUGHOR

CONGREGATIONS STAY TILL HALF-PAST-TWO IN THE MORNING

A remarkable religious revival is now taking place at Loughor. For some days a young man named Evan Roberts, a native of Loughor, has been causing great surprise at Moriah Chapel. The place has been besieged by dense crowds of people unable to obtain admission. Such excitement has prevailed that the road on which the chapel is situated has been lined with people from end to end. Roberts, who speaks in Welsh, opens his discourse by saying that he does not know what he is going to say but that when he is in communion with the Holy Spirit, the Holy Spirit will speak, and he will simply be the medium of His wisdom. The preacher soon launches out into a fervent and, at times, impassioned oration. His statements have had stirring effects upon his listeners. Many who have disbelieved Christianity for years are again returning to the fold of their younger days. One night, so great was the enthusiasm invoked by the young revivalist that, after his sermon which lasted two hours, the vast congregation remained praying and singing until two-thirty in the morning! Shopkeepers are closing early in order to get a place in the chapel, and tin and steel workers throng the place in their working clothes.

On November 11, Moriah was teeming with more than eight hundred people who were trying to squeeze into the little chapel. A young girl in her early teens seemed to capture the feeling when she cried out, "Oh, what will Heaven be like if it is so wonderful down here!"

By the next day, the prayer meetings had so over-flowed the chapel that people were opening their homes for meetings throughout the city. By early afternoon, wagons and carts were pouring into the town from all over the countryside. By night, even the home prayer meetings were overflowing as crowds stood outside, many of them straining to hear what was going on inside.

The evangelists were running from chapel to chapel and house to house. Salvation seemed to be flowing down the streets like a great flood. On this day, Sam Jenkins, the famous gospel singer, was first heard in the revival. In one of the galleries, he broke out in the song "Saved by Grace" and the multitude picked it up, singing it over and over. On this night, the great hymn "Throw Out the Lifeline" was also sung for the first time in the revival.

The meetings lasted until after 5 A.M. that Sunday morning. Evan introduced his friend Sydney to the throngs at Loughor and then departed for Aberdare without sleeping. The grocery shops were completely emptied of food as the people who had come from long distances determined that they were not going to go home. Feeling like they had found the cloud of glory, they were simply not going to leave it.

THE MEETINGS IN ABERDARE

On Sunday morning, November 13, Evan Roberts and five young ladies between the ages of eighteen and twenty (Priscilla Watkins, Mary Davies, Livina Hooker, Annie M. Rees, and Annie Davies) were driven to board the train at Swansea for Aberdare. These young girls were from nearby Gorseinon and had each been baptized in the Holy Spirit. They were about to carry the flame of revival all over Britain during the next eighteen months.

The opening meeting that Sunday in Aberdare was a disappointment. The local Christians criticized the youthfulness of the revival party, and it seemed that the Spirit was grieved. Even so, the young evangelists were not easily defeated. They were convinced that God had sent them to Aberdare, and therefore only God could send them away.

On the next evening, one thousand people crowded into the Ebenezer Congregational Chapel. Still there was no sign that the Lord was doing anything special. Even so, the next day almost the entire town stayed home from work to attend the morning prayer meeting. Inexplicably, with no one knowing how they were told, huge crowds were coming from all around the country. Anticipation was reaching a fever pitch even though nothing special had yet happened.

In the evening service, Evan Roberts circulated a hymn which was to become one of the great hymns of the revival: *Heavenly Jesus, ride victorious, Gird Thy sword upon Thy thigh.* There was a spontaneous outburst of worship, prayer, and praise. When this meeting was reaching its spiritual peak, Evan prophesied with great authority that a mighty revival was coming to *all* of Wales and they were only opening the gates for it. Before the meetings in Aberdare were to end, all of Britain would know that the Holy Spirit had indeed visited Wales.

THE FIRE SPREADS

From Aberdare, Evan traveled to more than two dozen cities and towns throughout Wales. In every place, the dry wood had been prepared and he simply cast the spark that would set it ablaze. The awe of the Lord was upon everyone, and His presence was felt everywhere. Spontaneous prayer meetings began in the mines, factories, schools, and shops. Even the amusement parks were filled with a holy awe as brigades of evangelists swept through them. Men who entered taverns to order drinks left them untouched as conviction and the fear of God came upon them.

Wave after wave of the Holy Spirit was passing over the land. The degree to which this move was affecting society could be seen in the way that it impacted the favorite Welsh sport, football (soccer). At the time the Welsh Revival broke out, the whole nation was nearly in a frenzy over the sport. Working-class men seemed to think and talk about this one obsession. Gambling on the games was rampant. Then the star football players were converted and joined the open-air street meetings to testify of the glorious things that the Lord had done for them. Soon the players were so captivated with the Lord that they lost interest in the games, the teams disbanded, and the stadiums sat empty unless used for the revival.

This miracle could only be compared to turning on your television set one Sunday afternoon to watch a National Football League game, only to hear the announcers trying to explain that none of the players had shown up because they were out evangelizing the city, and none of the fans had shown up because they were out there too! No one preached against sport or football—the people had simply become so passionate for the Lord that, for a season, such games just could no longer interest either the players or the people.

The degree to which Wales was impacted by this revival in such a short period of time does not have a counterpart anywhere in history. It was almost as if the nation had been converted in a day. Many considered it to be the best example in church history of how the Great Commission, to make disciples of nations, not just individuals, was to be fulfilled.

As the news spread about what was happening, men and women came from the far corners of the earth to witness it, and it does not seem that any were disappointed by what they found. Many testified of being profoundly impacted by the presence of the Lord as soon as they touched the soil of this little principality. Even letters and telegrams from Wales seemed to carry the fire. When they were opened and read, souls would be saved and revival would break out. No one had ever even heard of anything like this before, and it was just beginning!

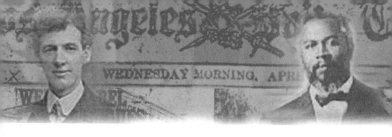

CHAPTER SIX

THE SILENT WEEK

For three months before the outburst of revival in Loughor, Evan Roberts had slept little as he continually interceded for his beloved Wales and sought a deeper communion with the Lord. This, too, seemed to be a key of the revival. Regardless of how great the revival fires burned, they kept praying for more.

During the months following the outbreak, Evan could scarcely find time to eat or sleep. Thousands of hungry new believers followed him everywhere he went. When we have taken the Lord's yoke and are working with Him, our labor actually refreshes us instead of tiring us, and men can experience superhuman endurance. However, even the Lord rested after His work of creation, and He established a principle that we should take regular rests from our labors. Evan had been going without rest for months, violating this principle. By the end of February 1905, he was near exhaustion.

God did not rest on the seventh day because He was weary; **"The Everlasting God, the Lord, the Creator of the ends of the earth does not become weary or tired" (Isaiah 40:28).** Neither does He call man to observe Sabbaths just for a cessation of labor, but rather for the purpose of drawing near to Him from whom our true sustenance comes. It was at this time that the Spirit revealed to Evan that he must have a week of silence.

On February 22, Evan revealed that he was not going to preach at Briton Ferry, where he had an engagement. For the entire week, he remained confined to his bedroom without speaking to anyone, not even his relatives. He was staying in the house of a Mr. and Mrs. Jones, who faithfully turned away hundreds of people, including famous preachers and newspaper men who had come from all over the world to see him.

This week of silence, just as the revival was reaching an unprecedented crescendo, amazed the world almost as much as the revival. How could the leader of such a move of God completely withdraw himself just as it was peaking? But Evan knew that he was not the source of the revival, and that if the presence of the Lord was removed, it would all end, regardless of how hard he and the other evangelists worked. Obedience is more important than sacrifice. Evan was willing to let the world's most famous preachers and reporters, who were all clamoring to see him, be offended rather than risk the Lord's displeasure. This is the foundation of true spiritual leadership. The greatest spiritual leader is the one who follows the Lord most closely, who fears the Lord more than men.

FOUR MORE PRINCIPLES

Evan did not reveal publicly what took place in his encounters with the Lord that week, but everyone noticed that he emerged from this period of isolation with an even greater anointing. In the personal diary he kept during this time, Evan noted on the fifth day, four simple principles to which he had to devote himself (which are to be distinguished from the four tenets for the revival; these were for Evan personally). They were, in his own words:

1) "I must take great care, first, to do all that God says—commands—and that only. Moses lost himself here—struck the rock."

2) "Second, to take every matter, however insignificant, to God in prayer. Joshua lost himself here: He made a covenant with the Gibeonites who pretended that they lived in a far-off country while they were living close at hand."

3) "Third, to give obedience to the Holy Spirit."

4) "Fourth, to give all the glory to Him."

On the sixth day of this week, Evan noted in his diary a personal prophecy from the Lord:

Lo, I am the Lord, who hath lifted thee up from the depth. I have sustained thee thus far. Lift up thine eyes and look on the fields and, behold, they are white. Shall I suffer thee to spread a table before Mine enemies? As I live, saith the Lord, the windows of heaven shall be opened, and the rain shall come down upon the parched earth. With flowers the wilderness shall yet be decked, and the meadow land shall be the habitation of kings. The ground shall sprout and blossom in its fullness and the heavens shall look down with laughter upon hidden riches on the earth, yielding glory unto God. Open thine hand, and I will fill it with power. Open thy mouth and I will fill it with wisdom. Open thy heart, and I will fill it with love. Look toward the west, and call thousands; toward the south, and say "Come," toward the north, and say "Draw nigh." Look towards the east and say "Let the sun arise and shed forth its warmth. Let life spring up. Let the nations which have rejected My name live." To kings turn thyself and say, "Bend;" To knights, "Submit ye." To the priests, "Deal out judgment, pity, forgiveness. Ye islands, seas, and kingdoms, give ear unto Me, I am the Almighty. Shall I lift up My rod over you? Did I not swear by the prophet Isaiah: **"I have sworn by myself, the word is gone out of my mouth in righteousness, and shall not return, that unto me every knee shall bow, every tongue shall swear?"** (Isaiah 45:23 KJV)

PROPHETIC OBEDIENCE

When Evan was later questioned by his friends concerning the principle object of what was called "The Silence," he explained: "It was not for the sake of my mind, or my body, to have a rest, but for *a sign*. When I asked the Lord what was the object of the seven days of silence, He distinctly said, 'As thy tongue was tied for seven days, so shall Satan be bound seven times.'"

Such prophetic signs are an enigma to the natural mind. When the king of Israel came to ask Elisha if he should fight against the Arameans, the prophet told him to strike the ground with his bow and arrows. When the king only struck the ground three times, the prophet was mad, declaring that if the king had struck the ground five or six times he would have destroyed his enemies. But because he only struck the ground three times, he would only defeat them three times (see II Kings 13:14-19). What did striking the ground with a bow and arrow have to do with the king's impending battles? Why were seven days of silence required of Evan Roberts for Satan to be bound seven times? The spiritual realm is *much greater* than the natural realm. Obedience to even the most seemingly insignificant promptings of the Spirit can have consequences in the spiritual realm that the natural mind just cannot comprehend.

Those who insist on understanding God's ways with their natural minds will trip over the spiritual stumbling blocks. The Lord warned us through Isaiah:

"For My thoughts are not your thoughts, neither are your ways My ways," declares the Lord.

"For as the heavens are higher than the earth, so are My ways higher than your ways, and My thoughts than your thoughts" (Isaiah 55:8-9).

Great moves of God require great obedience to the ways of the Spirit, but the flesh wars against the Spirit and many can never overcome this hurdle. Only the Spirit can beget that which is Spirit. Evan Roberts did not have to dress for power. He violated almost every church growth principle. He was neither educated nor eloquent. The only thing that he had going for him was the anointing. That was all he needed! Those who trust in the Spirit are utterly dependent on the Spirit. If the Holy Spirit did not show up, Evan had nothing else to fall back on. He did not have a program he could resort to or leftover sermons he could warm up.

When we have only the Holy Spirit, then obedience to the Spirit is everything. Few have ever been so willing to trust in the Lord to this degree, and few have ever seen true revival because of it. If the Lord does not show up at our meetings, we usually have a pretty good program anyway. It is not wrong to have a plan or a program, unless they are used as a substitute for the Spirit.

As one famous evangelist once said, "If the Lord completely departed from many churches, they would not ever realize it." But those who have tasted of His presence can never again be satisfied with mere programs—they must have the Lord.

Even though the hype, manipulation, and many programs instituted as a substitute for the lack of anointing have wearied the church to the degree that the Laodicean spirit of lukewarmness now pervades, there is a hunger for the Lord Himself that is beginning to rise again. The church at the end of this age will return to her first love. She will be so compelled to draw near to Him that He will draw near to her—on a scale that will signify that even this great Welsh Revival was but a foretaste of what is to come.

CHAPTER SEVEN

THE WORKERS AND THE WORSHIP

During the Welsh Revival, people loved and honored the evangelists and workers, but they came to the meetings for God. They crowded chapels to overflowing, not even knowing whether an evangelist would be there or not. Sometimes Evan Roberts would enter a meeting and sit on the front seat and say nothing for three hours. Then he would stand up, preach, and/or pray for some ten or fifteen minutes and sit down. At times, he might preach or pray the whole time. At other times, he would sit silently through the entire meeting. Regardless of what Evan did, the people would carry on under the influence of the Holy Spirit.

There were soloists, duos, and special singers during the revival, but they seldom announced where they were going to sing. Sometimes they went to a place expecting to sing, but the Spirit had other plans, and they would keep their peace or they might just pray. Those who witnessed their ministry only had the witness that when they did sing, it *was* the Holy Spirit.

This was a revival in which the Lord Jesus Christ Himself was the center and the main attraction. "It was noised abroad that HE was in the house." The young workers knew that the Holy Spirit came to testify of Jesus, and if an evangelist or the evangelistic party became the center of the attraction, then they would miss the real power and potential of the Holy Spirit in that meeting.

Evan Roberts knew that he was popular, but he dreaded publicity. He felt that it detracted from the One who was the true Source of the Welsh Revival. He dreaded newspaper reporters, not because they were skeptics and cynics as they tend to be today, but because he dreaded their adulation!

Many times, Evan withdrew himself from the meetings when he felt that the people were coming to see and hear him instead of coming for the Lord. In meetings where he felt he was the center of attraction, he pleaded with an agonized spirit for the people to look away to Christ and Him alone, or else the Holy Spirit would withdraw Himself from them.

Though Evan Roberts became the most publicized preacher in the world at that time, he often refused interviews with reporters, even when they came from the opposite ends of earth. He refused to be photographed except by members of his own family. He continually repeated that this awakening was from God, not from himself, and that if people idolized him the glory would be withdrawn. He did not even answer the multitude of requests that came from publishing houses around the world seeking to write his biography. He greatly feared that by doing this, he might rob the Lord of even some of the glory that was due only to Him.

To Speak or Not to Speak

Being led by the Spirit requires knowing when not to speak as much as when to speak. Evan Roberts was a wonderful demonstration of this sensitivity to the Lord. During a meeting he would often sit among the people without saying a word. Visitors from different parts of the world were astonished as they observed him letting the course of crowded gatherings be dictated entirely by the people's sensitivity to the Spirit as they sang, prayed, and testified.

F.B. Meyer, a renowned Christian leader of the time, upon watching Evan Roberts in the meetings explained, "He will not go in front of the divine Spirit, but is willing to stand aside and remain in the background unless he is perfectly sure that the Spirit of God is moving him." Then he added, "It is a profound lesson for us all!" The one who knows when not to speak will speak with more authority when he does.

Christian leaders who had come from the four corners of the earth stood in awe and bowed in adoration to God as they witnessed the revival. General William Booth, Gypsy Smith, F.B. Meyer, G. Campbell Morgan, and many other renowned men and women of God came to marvel at this great visitation. In most cases, they only prayed or said a few words. Sometimes they sat quietly in the meetings while young people, and even children prayed, sang, and testified in the Spirit. The men of God who all came quickly recognized that this was not a revival that came through great preachers or great preaching—this was a supernatural work, altogether apart from either.

To their credit, most of these men quickly understood that their very personalities would actually hinder the meetings, and they yielded to the Holy Spirit. Great preaching is loved by all who love the Word of God, but these great preachers knew that their preaching had never produced the kind of presence of the Lord they encountered in Wales.

CHILDREN ENTER THE KINGDOM

We are seeing in our own times a great movement to equip and train the children and youth in the ways of the Lord, and to see even the very young as vital members of the body of Christ. This movement is from the Lord and it is significant, but the Welsh Revival was quite different. In Wales, it was the children and youth who sought to equip their parents and train the adults in the ways of the Lord. The Lord said that we had to become like little children to enter the kingdom—they may have more to teach us than we have to teach them!

Evan Roberts was only in his mid-twenties when the revival broke out. His sister, Mary, who was such an important part of the work, was sixteen. Their brothers Dan, and Mary's future husband, Sydney Evans, were both about twenty. The "Singing Sisters," who were greatly used, were between the ages of eighteen and twenty-two.

Thousands of young people were converted and immediately spread over the land, testifying to the glory of God. Little children had their own prayer meetings and witnessed boldly even to the most hardened sinners. The chapels overflowed with the young.

THE WORSHIP

Spontaneous worship that gives birth to a new form of worship is usually found in true revivals. This was also true of the Welsh Revival. This probably could not have happened had there been just one strong worship leader in the revival. There were strong worship leaders present, but they yielded, understanding that this revival was not for the purpose of birthing new superstars, but to glorify Jesus. This allowed the Holy Spirit to give birth to new songs and even a new form of worship that had not been previously known.

Much of the contemporary style of worship that is now attributed to either the Pentecostal or Charismatic movements actually had its origin in Wales. One of the great contributions of the Welsh Revival was the new spontaneous form of worship called "singing in the Spirit" that was to become a signature of the Holy Spirit's presence for decades to come. R.B. Jones, a leader in the revival, said of the music:

> *The fact is, unless heard, it is unimaginable and when heard indescribable. There was no hymnbook. No one gave out a hymn. Just anyone would start the singing, and very rarely did it happen that the hymn started was out of harmony with the mood at the moment. Once started, as if moved by a simultaneous*

impulse, the hymn was caught up by the whole congregation almost as if what was about to be sung had been announced and all were responding to the baton of a visible human leader. I have seen nothing like it. You felt that the thousand or fifteen hundred persons before you had become merged into one myriad-headed, but simple-souled personality. Such was the perfect blending of the mood and purpose that it bore eloquent testimony to a unity created only by the Spirit of God. Another witness testified: "The praying and singing were both wonderful. There was no need for an organ. The assembly was its own organ as a thousand sorrowing or rejoicing hearts found expression in the Psalmody of their native hills."

THEY KNEW HOW TO CARRY THE ARK

The ark of the covenant represented God's presence to the ancient nation of Israel. There are many great lessons in the Old Testament stories of the ark concerning how we should and should not treat the presence of the Lord. When the ark was treated as holy and carried before them into battle, great and miraculous victories were won. When the ark was not treated as holy, but used as a good luck charm, they lost the battle and the ark, as it was captured by their enemies.

One of the greatest reasons why the Welsh Revival burned so brightly, and for so long, is that the leaders knew how to carry the "ark" of God's presence. They knew how to remain open and submitted to the Lord's leading and how not to offend the Spirit. Those who were used so mightily in this revival were loathe to say anything that might draw attention to themselves and away from the Savior.

As Psalm 25:14 states, **"The secret of the Lord is for those who fear Him...."** They wanted to be close enough to Him to know His deepest secrets, so they learned to respect Him properly. Combined with their great love for the Lord, they had a profound and holy fear of offending Him. They loved the ark of His presence and could not be content without having it with them, but they also reverenced it enough to learn how to handle it properly.

In this great awakening, there was no ministry building, no boasting in men—only the Lord. When the glory of the Lord really does rest on an earthen vessel, it is not the vessel that receives the attention! We must heed Peter's warning: **"Therefore humble yourselves under the mighty hand of God, that He may exalt you at the proper time" (I Peter 5:6 NASU).** Again, it is our job to humble ourselves; it is God's job to exalt. If we try to do His job, He will do our job!

Because the leaders of the Welsh Revival were so committed to humbling themselves, God could exalt them. They refused to send out newsletters to build their own ministries, so the Lord used the front page of almost every major newspaper in the world to spread the word of what He was doing in Wales. As soon as He found the people humble enough to handle His promotion, He gave it to them.

We can build influence by self-promotion, but God will promote only those who do not promote themselves. That which is built on self-promotion will have to be maintained by human striving. Those who allow God to build the house have taken a yoke that is easy and a burden that is light. Those who allow God to build the work will not be worn-out by the work, but will be refreshed in it.

No man can tear down that which God builds. When we are doing the work of God, we do not carry the worries and fears that those who have built on self-promotion must carry. **"Everything that God does will remain forever" (see Ecclesiastes 3:14).** The fruit of the work that God initiates will remain. The work that is built on self-promotion inevitably ends in tragedy and disappointment. Though it is apparent that the high state of the Welsh Revival itself did not last, some of the fruit of it did. It was able to impart to the universal church many of the ways of God that remain to this day.

When revival itself becomes our goal, it is seldom attained because it becomes an idol. Revival must never become an end in itself, but a means to an even higher end—the glory of the Lord being revealed and His kingdom being extended. Sometimes His kingdom is extended by other means than revival.

Certainly we need more true revivals, but even those are founded upon simple obedience to whatever His plan may be, and His whole plan does not revolve just around revival. The day-to-day obedience of the church, and growing in true spiritual maturity, is just as important to the fulfillment of God's purposes as the great outbreaks of revival. When the cloud of His presence lifts and begins to move, we must be ready to move with Him. But when the cloud does not move, it is just as important that we rest in Him.

CHAPTER EIGHT

THEY PRAYED AND SAVED SOULS

There is a complaint among many evangelists that those who call themselves intercessors seldom do anything of substance. There is often a similar accusation from the intercessors that the other ministries do not pray enough. Both may be true at times. However, those with accomplishments would probably not accomplish nearly as much without those who are praying for them, and those who are praying would not have their prayers answered if it were not for those who responded to the Holy Spirit to be used by Him. In the Welsh Revival, and indeed almost every true revival, there is a wonderful combination of prayer and works. In fact, those who prayed the most were also those who tended to do the most in this revival.

Without question, the Welsh Revival was birthed and carried by a devotion to prayer and intercession. This was to be one of the great contributions as it soon spread throughout the worldwide Christian community. Much of the fire that continues in some of the great prayer movements of today could likely trace their origin to the fires lit in the Welsh Revival. The prayer and the praise mingled together in most of the meetings. James E. Stewart wrote:

It was praying that rent the heavens; praying that received direct answers there and then. The spirit of intercession was so mightily poured out that the whole congregation would take part simultaneously for hours! Strangers were startled to hear the young and unlettered pray with such unction and intelligence as they were swept up to the Throne of Grace by the Spirit of God. Worship and adoration was unbounded. Praise began to mingle with the petitions as answered prayer was demonstrated before their very eyes. Often when unsaved loved ones were the focus of the intercession, they would be compelled to come to the very meeting and be saved!

This fed the fires further for both the worship and the intercession. When the believers understood that God really did hear their prayers, prayer quickly rose to the highest priority in their lives. As they prayed with more faith, they began to see quick answers to them. When they became increasingly specific in their requests, the answers became even more spectacular. They would pray for specific friends or family members in one meeting, and that person would be at the altar seeking salvation in the next one. This would fan the flames of intercession even more. This unquestionably fanned the flames of the revival.

Prayer meetings, which had before been drudgery, became the main attractions, even for entire towns. Meetings swelled until overflowing, both with people and with the anointing. Meetings that were expected to be regular services quickly became prayer meetings, as it became the first nature of everyone to pray. Groups walking to work would start praying, and soon they would be joined by a swelling crowd who was drawn by the anointing.

Spontaneous prayer meetings started in shops, homes, and there were even cases when factories shut down so that the workers could pray. At the peak of the revival, whole populations of towns were gathering to march around their neighborhoods and claim them for Christ. On several occasions, the population of a town would march to a neighboring town to pray for it, and the revival would inevitably be ignited there. This revival was a witness that few things can so energize believers as when they discover the power of prayer.

THEY SAVED SOULS

The main focus of prayer in this revival was always for the lost. There can be no revival without soul-winning, and in saving lost souls the Welsh Revival must be considered one of the most intense and effective revivals of all time. Yet, there did not seem to be any messages or meetings that were devoted to just evangelism. The salvations mostly came because of the fire that was on all of the believers at the time.

This revival was not a program for using a few preachers or a campaign to get church members testifying to the saving grace of the Lord Jesus. There were no classes given on how to reach the lost. It just seemed like every Christian in Wales erupted simultaneously with a burning agony for the lost. The joy of salvation simply could not be contained by the believers as every coal mine, tramcar, office, school, or shop became a pulpit for the gospel.

Even more than the preaching, it was the witness of the common believers which led multiplied thousands to a saving faith in Jesus. There was no set pattern of strategy for the witnessing; it was simply born out of an overflowing joy and faith that could not be contained in those who knew the Savior.

The presence of the Lord was so intense in Wales that those who had traveled from the ends of the earth, at a time when this took weeks or months, simply to witness the revival, said that just being in one of the revival meetings was worth the whole journey—even if Evan and Dan Roberts or Sydney Evans were not there.

Methodists claimed that it was a revival of the Wesley meetings of a century before. The people of Wales lost a lot of sleep because they were afraid that if they left the services they would miss something wonderful. The meetings carried on until two and three o'clock in the morning many times, and did not end until the people, sometimes including the entire population of a city or town, had marched through the streets singing the praises of the Lamb of God!

It was simply impossible for an unbeliever to escape this overpowering witness, or not to be drawn into it by the sheer love and zeal of the people. Just as it is easy to identify a man or a woman who is in love, as their lover dominates their minds and conversation, Wales fell so in love with Jesus that adoration for Him lifted His name above anything else that could capture the people's attention. The knowledge of the Lord simply washed over Wales just as the waters cover the sea. As Jesus was lifted up, all men came.

The ultimate goal of Evan Roberts and his little band, who were considered the main fire-starters and carriers of the revival, was for one hundred thousand souls to come to Christ in Wales. This number was surpassed in just the first three months, and the ultimate number saved in Wales alone likely reached several times that number. But because the people and workers were so focused on the Lord and not just the fruit, no one kept numbers of conversions. Many more were brought to salvation throughout the British Isles, and it is simply impossible to estimate the number who gave their lives to Christ throughout the world as a direct result of the fires of revival in Wales.

As the Great Commission is to make disciples of all nations, not just individuals, the Welsh Revival is without peer in transforming a nation with the Gospel. As we will read, this was done on a level that few would probably ever consider possible if it had not been done here. It did become the standard by which all other revivals to date have been measured, and to date none yet has ever measured up to it in many ways—but they will!

Chapter Nine

THE WORLD MARVELED

Almost every great revival or move of God in both Scripture and history was ignited by a single individual, but none of them were sustained by just one individual. The same was true in Wales. Almost everyone recognized that Evan Roberts was the principal individual used to both start and sustain the revival. But as we covered, there were many others who were used to prepare the nation for it, and others still who fanned the flames throughout the nation. It was not the presence of Evan Roberts which brought revival, but the presence of God.

Even the greatest vessel that the Lord uses is still an "earthen vessel." Once we behold the glory of the Lord, the vessel loses our attention. Compared to the Lord Jesus, even the great Apostle Paul is a mere man, an empty vessel. But very few have ever risen above worshiping the temple of the Lord, so that they can truly worship the Lord of the temple.

The reporters and preachers who flocked to Wales from around the world all wanted to see Evan Roberts. Those who were a part of the revival hardly even noticed when Evan entered a meeting. They loved and respected him, but their hearts were captured by the glory of the Son of God. Because the people had fallen in love with the Lord, they therefore loved and honored His messengers, but they did not worship them. When we see the glory of the Son, it is impossible to be overly impressed by men, whether they are kings, presidents, or even the greatest men of God.

Evan Roberts was a yielded vessel whom the Lord could use, but so were a multitude of other pastors and evangelists who were used to reap a mighty harvest simultaneously with the ministry of Evan and Dan Roberts, Sydney Evans, Sam Jenkins, and "The Singing Sisters." The revival spread to the uttermost points of Wales although the principal evangelists never visited there. The Welsh Revival is a study of the Lord's use of sovereign vessels, and how He sometimes chooses to move sovereignly without any vessels at all. The Lord never limits Himself to move only according to one plan.

THE COMMON DENOMINATOR

There was a conspicuous common denominator found everywhere that this revival broke out. It was that the Son of God was being lifted up, and all men were being drawn to Him. Holiness and obedience were emphasized, but it was primarily because the Son was holy and everyone wanted to please Him in all things.

The presence of the Lord was so strong that no one could imagine speaking vile words or performing vile acts in His presence.

Those who were present could only describe His presence as being absolutely beyond description! The promptings of the Holy Spirit were so distinct that thousands would simultaneously spring to their feet to worship in such perfect unison that those who witnessed it considered it miraculous. At times, the glory of the Lord would so shine from the pulpit that the evangelist or pastor would flee from it to keep from being completely overcome. Many testified that they could not stand the brightness of the glory of the Lord that came upon some meetings, physically and visibly.

Thousands of young converts spread out all over the land preaching the good news they had found. They had no credentials or authority from men—all they had was the Holy Spirit and that was all they needed. The Book of Acts was happening all over again, and then some. Small children won many souls for Christ. New converts were leading large prayer meetings and Bible studies. At times, Bible studies or prayer meetings being held in the same city would all empty into the streets at the same time, following an unseen Conductor, marching around the town together singing praises to the Lord until the early morning hours.

The largest and most influential newspapers were soon almost completely dominated by news of the revival. Headlines of crime, violence, and scandal were replaced by conversion counts, news from the meetings, the words to new hymns, and revival maps detailing where the Spirit was moving with the greatest intensity. The advertisements for liquor disappeared, and the large advertisements were all bought by Christian publishers trying to keep up with the need for Bibles and hymnbooks.

The following reports were compiled by James E. Stewart from a newspaper under the heading *Doings of the Churches* and published in his book *Invasion of Wales by the Spirit*:

BLAENAVON. On Saturday evening, a band of young lads between the ages of fourteen and sixteen held prayer meetings in the different places in the principal streets.

DOWLAIS. At a recent prayer meeting, attended by no fewer than 214 persons, the proceedings resolved themselves into a huge Bible class. This great interest in the Holy Scriptures is the result of the present revival.

BRYNCETHIN. The services have now been held here nightly for fifteen weeks and a large number of converts have been added to the Free Churches. For the sake of educating the young converts, it has been decided to have a Bible class for two nights in every week and these classes are very largely attended.

RHOS. Visitors to the revival meeting continue to pour in from the Lake District, Birkenhead, Liverpool, and the adjoining districts.

TREMADOC. The revival has had and continues to have a marked effect here. The chapels have been overflowing up to two and three o'clock in the morning.

NEWBRIDGE. An official of the Colynen colliery, when asked how the religious fervor had expressed itself underground, said: "This is a blessed time. When I go around on my inspection now I rarely hear a blasphemous word of oath. There is a glorious change for the better."

CARDIGAN. A meeting in the Tabernacle Calvinist Methodist Church where the Rev. Seth Joshua was conducting a mission was prolonged till after midnight. It was a wonderful gathering and will long be remembered for the outpouring of the Holy Spirit. Most of the 1,200 people present were on their knees simultaneously, and they remained in this attitude for about two hours and many persons are known to have accepted Christ.

HOLYHEAD. In this important town, a drunken man is a thing of the past and the police are having an easy time of it. 500 converts have been reported.

PONTYPOOL. The missionary enthusiasm is running high amongst the 200 converts at the Tabernacle and at a recent meeting it was decided to divide them into groups and to hold services at different cottages.

Street disturbances have become conspicuous by their absences and the fact that there has not been a single fight at the bottom of High Street, which is always regarded as the "prize ring of

Pontypool," is put down to the good influences of the Revival.

COEDPOETH. This quiet neighborhood has felt a strong spiritual visitation for the past three months. The total number of converts is now 210 and many more are expected. There have been united prayer meetings three nights a week and on the rest of the evenings each church holds meetings at its own place of worship. Remarkable scenes have been witnessed. The women have daily prayer meetings, morning and evening. Young men and young women are preaching in the open air with great success and many drunkards have been converted. The life of whole churches has been reformed.

BLAENAVON. All the churches in the town recently had a combined procession through the streets and now a second parade has been arranged.

ABERTILLERY. As the result of the special week of meetings there have been about 1,500 converts.

BRITHOIR. A meeting near the railway station—the continuation of a previous prayer meeting — was attended by many persons from clubs and public houses and continued until near midnight. Then they went to the nearby Chapel and the gathering broke up at 2 A.M.

AMMANFORD. Half a dozen young people cannot meet accidentally in the street without joining in praise. Recently a group of children met on The Cross and began to sing and pray.

Ultimately they were joined by men and women and the result was a grand open air prayer meeting. Ammanford is a new town. Young people, full of enthusiasm, frequently walk three or four miles over the mountains to villages, farms, and hamlets to hold meetings.

TREHARRIS. At Brynhyfrd Welsh Baptist, forty candidates were recently baptized making a total of 138 baptisms. 220 have recently been saved in this church.

RHONDDA VALLEY. A scene which may be witnessed any morning in dozens of pits in South Wales is carried out every morning here at 5 A.M. Scores of miners hold a service before going home from the midnight shift. The Superintendent starts a hymn, "In the deep and mighty ocean," and then the pit echoes the song. An old man whose grey head is tinged with coal dust falls on his knees to pray. Others do the same. The service attracts men from different workings and flickering lights are seen approaching the improvised temple. "Now, boys, those of you who love Christ, UP WITH YOUR LAMP!" cries a young miner. In a second, scores of lights flicker in the air and another song of thanks sets the mine ringing.

ABERTILLERY (again). The work goes on. Great things have taken place in the Salvation Army Hall but services are held nightly in practically every chapel in the neighborhood. There are now 2,500 converts.

ANGLESEY. The Isle of Anglesey has been stirred from end to end by the revival. At the 55 Methodist chapels there have been 1,116 converts, 276 at 15 Independent chapels, 366 at the 24 Baptist places of worship, and 116 at the 8 Wesleyan Churches, making a total of 1,673 converts for the 102 chapels.

CAERNARFON. A score of volunteer missionaries numbering 150 from the local churches of the town have undertaken house to house visitation to invite the people to come to the churches.

REVIVAL FERVOR IN DURHAM, (England). Revival fervor still spreads in North West Durham in the North of England. Those connected with the cause for a long period remember no such general awakening during the last 20 years. There has been an upheaval which has been the general topic of conversation throughout the whole district. All over Durham marvelous scenes are taking place, and the chapels are packed every night with souls being saved.

GARW VALLEY. Underground meetings are being held in nearly all the collieries. The early converts are among the most ardent workers and their efforts are proving very successful. At one of these underground meetings, no fewer than 36 men surrendered themselves to Christ.

GARNDIFFAITH. At Pisgah, 40 conversions are recorded. A man 70 years of age stood up and confessed Christ as his Savior. Although late, he felt that he was glad that he had at last found peace and joy. A young man had been praying for his father and he asked that his petition might be answered that night. Just then his father came to the meeting and made a full surrender. A man who had been a great drunkard and blasphemer and who had starved his wife and children by missing his work for weeks at a time, found his way into one of the meetings and, with tears streaming from his eyes, he cried aloud for forgiveness. He prayed that God might find a way to his wife's heart and she, too, soon cried for pardon. Shouts of praise and joy were raised.

GLYNNEATH. The two independent churches ADDOLDY and CAPEL-Y-GLYN which had been on unbrotherly terms for a period of nearly twelve years have been reconciled and united meetings have been held. The two ministers shook hands before a united church of nearly 400 members.

HAFOD. Underground prayer meetings at the Trevor pit have been conducted by Mr. W. Rogers, who is known as the converted footballer.

PENTRE. The ministers of all the chapels recently exchanged pulpits for a day with the idea of breaking down denominationalism.

MAESTEG. An insurance agent told a reporter that at practically every house he called at after Christmas he was met by the wife with a happy smile and these words, "This is the happiest Christmas we have ever had." Their husbands had been converted and stopped their wastage of money in gambling and drunkenness.

CAERNAFON. Details have just reached us of wonderful meetings. The influence of the Holy Spirit is felt most powerfully by men and women alike. Strong men pale and tremble. Young men and women storm the gates of heaven with overwhelming importunity and overpowering effect. The whole congregation is completely melted into pronounced weeping and sobbing. Large numbers are finding the Lord. Two well known reprobates came forward and sank on their knees and began to beat their breasts.

The Bible Society's records show that over three times the number of Bibles are now being sold since the revival broke out. The booksellers say it is no trouble now to sell Bibles; the trouble is to get them.

A lovely story is told of a child of four in an infant class who held up his hand to call the teacher's attention. "Well?" inquired the teacher, "What is it?" Swift and telling came the words, "Please, teacher, do you love Jesus?" The arrow reached its mark. There and then the teacher came to the Lord and she later went out to India as a missionary. Someone overheard one child ask another, "Do you know what has happened at Rhos?" "No, I don't, except that Sunday comes every day now!"

"Don't you know?" "No, I don't." "Why, Jesus Christ has come to live in Rhos, now."

Winkey Pratney found and recorded the following newspaper report in his book, *Revival* (Whitaker House, pages 190-191):

The scene is almost indescribable. Tier upon tier of men and women filled every inch of space. Those who could not gain admittance stood outside and listened at the doors. Others rushed to the windows where almost every word was audible. When at 7:00 the service began, 2,000 people must have been present. The enthusiasm was unbounded. Women stood and shouted until perspiration ran down their faces, and then jumped up one after another to testify. One told in quivering accents the story of a drunken life. A working collier spoke like a practiced orator; one can imagine what a note the testimony of a converted gypsy woman struck when, dressed in her best, she told of her reformation and repentance. At ten o'clock the meeting had lost none of its ardor. Prayer after prayer went up . . . time and again the four ministers who stood in the pulpit attempted to start a hymn, but it was all in vain. The revival has taken hold of the people, and even Mr. Roberts cannot keep it in check. His latest convert is a policeman who, after complaining that the people had gone mad after religion so there was nothing to do, went to see for himself, and bursting into tears, confessed the error of his ways and repented.

William T. Stead, the editor of the famous *Pall Mall Gazette* was thought by some to be the most powerful man in Britain at the time. He made a personal visit to the revival and the *London Methodist Times* recorded the following interview with him upon his return (published in *The Great Revival in Wales*, Shaw, page 56):

"Well, Mr. Stead, you've been to the revival. What do you think of it?"

"Sir," Mr. Stead replied, "the question is not what I think of it, but what it thinks of me, of you, and all the rest of us. For it is a very real thing, this revival, a live thing which seems to have a power and a grip which may get hold of a good many of us who at present are mere spectators."

"Do you think it is on the march then?"

"A revival is something like a revolution. It is apt to be wonderfully catching."

"You speak as if you dreaded the revival coming your way."

"No, that is not so. Dread is not the right word. Awe expresses my sentiment better. For you are in the presence of the unknown. You have read ghost stories and can imagine what you would feel if you were alone at midnight in the haunted chamber of some old castle and you heard the slow and stealthy step stealing along the corridor where the visitor from another world was said to walk. If you go to South Wales and watch the revival, you will feel pretty much just like that. There is something there from the other world. You cannot say whence it came or whither it is going, but it moves and lives and reaches for you all the time. You see men and women go down in sobbing agony before your eyes as the invisible Hand clutches at their heart. and you shudder. It is pretty grim I tell you, if you are afraid of strong emotions, you'd better give the revival a wide berth."

"But is it all emotion? Is there no teaching?"

"Precious little. Do you think teaching is what people want in revival? These people, all the people in a land like ours are taught to death, preached to insensibility. They all know the essential truths. They know they are not living as they ought to live, and no amount of teaching will add anything to that conviction."

"Then I take it your net impressions have been favorable?"

"How could they be otherwise? Did I not feel the pull of that unseen Hand? Have I not heard the glad outburst of melody that hailed the confession of some who in a very truth had found salvation? Of course it is all very much like what I have seen in the Salvation Army. And I was delighted to see that at last the Welsh churches are recognizing the equal ministry of men and women. . . There is a wonderful spontaneity about it all, and so far its fruits have been good and only good."

"Will it last?"

"Nothing lasts forever in this mutable world. . . but if the analogy of all previous revivals holds good, this religious awakening will be influencing for good the lives of numberless men and women who will be living and toiling and carrying on with this God's world of ours long after you and I have been gathered to our fathers."

Even the most powerful politicians, statesmen, intellectuals, and rival religious leaders had difficulty denying the impact of the revival on the entire principality of Wales. Debts were paid, stolen goods returned, and the taverns were forsaken and closed. A serious problem developed at the mines because the horses had been trained to respond to commands that were curses from the drivers, and since drivers did not curse anymore, the horses could not understand their commands!

Political meetings were postponed because the members of Parliament were in the revival meetings. Theatrical companies quit going to Wales because no one would attend their shows. Magistrates were presented with white gloves in many towns to signify that there were *no* arrests. The prisons were emptied. Revival scenes swept the universities day after day for months. Over seventy thousand names of new converts were reported in the papers in just two months.

CHAPTER TEN
THEY FOLLOWED THE SPIRIT

T ime constraints in the meetings were forgotten. Announced to begin at a certain hour, people would gather hours before. No one knew when the services would end and clocks were simply ignored. Meetings began as soon as part of the congregation had assembled because the people seldom waited for a human leader. There has possibly never been a religious movement so little indebted to the guiding minds of its leaders.

When the evening meeting, which began at seven o'clock, poured out at three o'clock the next morning, other crowds were already preparing to get into the chapel for the early morning prayer meeting! In many towns all work ceased when the evangelists came. The factories and shops would sometimes close for days at a time so the people could attend the meetings.

A famous reporter of the great *London Daily* visited the meetings of the young prophet of Loughor in order to describe to the people in London the amazing scenes about which they had heard. He wrote:

I found the flame of Welsh religious enthusiasm as smokeless as its coal. There are no advertisements, no brass bands, no posters. All the paraphernalia of the got-up job (typical meetings) are conspicuous by their absence. There is no instrumental music. The pipe organs lie unused. There is no need of instruments for in and around and beneath surge the all-prevailing thrill and throb of a multitude praying, and singing as they pray.

The vast congregations are soberly sane, as orderly and at least as reverent as any congregation I ever saw beneath the dome of St. Paul's cathedral. Tier above tier in the crowded aisle to the loftiest gallery sit or stand as necessity dictates, eager hundreds of serious men and thoughtful women, their eyes riveted upon the platform or upon whatever part of the building is the storm center of the meeting. The vast majority of the congregation are stalwart young miners.

"We must obey the Spirit" is the watchword of Evan Roberts, and he is as obedient as the humblest of his audience. No one uses a hymnbook; no one gives out a hymn. The last person to control the meeting in any way is Evan Roberts. You feel that the thousand or fifteen hundred persons before you have become merged into one myriad-headed but single-souled personality. You can watch what they call "the influence of the power of the Spirit" playing over

the congregation as an ebbing wind plays over the surface of the pond.

A very remarkable instance of this abandonment of the meeting to the spontaneous impulse, not merely of those within the walls but of those crowded outside, who were unable to get in, occurred on Sunday night. Twice the order of proceeding, if order it can be called, was altered by the crowd outside who, by some mysterious impulse started a hymn on their own account which was at once taken up by the congregation within. On one of these occasions Evan Roberts was addressing the meeting. He at once gave way and the singing became general.

The meeting always breaks out into a compassionate and consoling song, until the soloist, having recovered his breath, rises from his knees and sings a song.

The praying and singing are both wonderful. But more impressive than either are the breaks which occur when utterance can be no more, and then the sobbing in the silence momentarily heard is drowned in tempest of melody. No need for an organ. The assembly is its own organ as a thousand or fifteen hundred sorrowing or rejoicing hearts find expression in the sacred Psalmody of their native hills.

Repentance, open confession, intercessory prayer, and above all else this marvelous musical liturgy—a liturgy unwritten, but heartfelt mighty chorus rising like the thunder of the surge of the rock-bound shore, ever and anon broken by the flute-like note of the singing sisters whose melody is as sweet and as spontaneous as the music of the throstle in the grove or the martin in the skies. And all this vast quivering, throbbing, singing, praying, exultant multitude intensely conscious of the all-pervading influence of some invisible reality—now for the first time moving palpable though not tangible in their midst. They call it THE SPIRIT OF GOD.

THE CROSS WAS THE CENTER

The following recorded prayer of Evan Roberts captures succinctly the central emphasis and devotion of the revival evangelists:

Lord Jesus, help us now through the Holy Spirit to come face to face with the cross. Whatever the hindrances may be, we commit the service to Thee. Put us all under the Blood. Oh, Lord, place the Blood on all our past up to this moment. We thank Thee for the Blood. In the Name of Jesus Christ, bind the devil this moment. We point to the Cross of Christ. It is our Cross and we take its conquest.

Reveal the Cross through the Name of Jesus. Oh, open the Heavens. Descend upon us now. Tear open our hearts; give us such a sight of Calvary that our hearts may be broken. Oh Lord, descend now; open our hearts to receive the heart that bled for us. If we are to be fools—make us fools for Thee. Take us, spirit, soul, and body. WE ARE THINE. Thou hast purchased us.

Reveal the Cross for the sake of Jesus—the Cross that is to conquer the world. Place us under the

Blood. Forbid that we should think of what men may say of us. Oh speak—speak—speak, Lord Jesus. Thy Words are "wine indeed." Oh, reveal the Cross, beloved Jesus—the Cross in its glory.

Reign in every heart for the sake of Jesus. Lord, do Thou help us to see the dying Savior. Enable us to see Him conquering the hosts of darkness. Claim victory for Thy Son, now Lord. He is worthy to have the victory. THOU ART THE ALL-POWERFUL GOD. OH, CLAIM VICTORY. We shall give all the glory to Thy Name. No one else has a right to the glory but Thee. Take it, Lord. Glorify Thy Son in this meeting. OH, HOLY SPIRIT—DO THOU WORK THROUGH US AND IN US NOW. Speak Thy Word in power for Thy Name's sake. Amen—and Amen!

The love, sufferings, death, and resurrection of Jesus were the theme of every meeting, every sermon, every prayer, and became the passion of every heart. The people were not being converted to a new doctrine, denomination, personality, or even the new movement— they were converted to Jesus. The leaders of the revival held steadfast to the exhortation of the Apostle Paul, who said:

And when I came to you, brethren, I did not come with superiority of speech or of wisdom, proclaiming to you the testimony of God.

For I determined to know nothing among you except Jesus Christ, and Him crucified (I Corinthians 2:1-2).

Conversions in the Welsh Revival were not just temporarily changed people who were caught up in the excitement—they were so radically changed that being "born again" was not just a cliché—it was a reality. The new believers' first encounter with the Lord was not the promise of blessings; it was a profound comprehension of their own sinful condition and their desperate need for the Savior. When moved by the Spirit to open the wells of salvation, they did not just raise their hands in the back of the building to acknowledge their "decision," they were racked with such a holy desperation for the mercy of the Savior that they tumbled to the floor as if in physical pain.

Those under conviction would sometimes writhe in their own tears until they gained the assurance of forgiveness. Then their grief would turn into a joy of an equal depth that would be impossible to contain. As the meetings began to disband, often at two or three in the morning, new converts just could not leave and would continue singing, praying, and at times laughing uncontrollably until the prayer meetings started at sunrise.

CHAPTER ELEVEN

A NATION IS BORN AGAIN

The effects of the revival on the nation of Wales are unique in history. The First and Second Great Awakenings undoubtedly changed the genetic codes of Britain and America profoundly, but history simply reveals no other examples where the changes in society equaled what happened in Wales in such a short period of time.

Some of the cities and towns that had been on the brink of anarchy, with violent crimes increasing out of control, did not record a single arrest during the revival. This was one of the most lawless regions. Others would record but one or two for such crimes as drunkenness in public over the two year period of the revival. Many of the jails and prisons were completely empty.

Before the revival there had been a plague of drunkenness and gambling. During the revival, taverns were either closed or turned into meeting halls. Instead of wasting their earnings on drinking and gambling, workers started taking their wages home to their families. Because of the conviction of the Holy Spirit, restitution became a fruit of repentance, and outstanding debts were being paid by thousands of young converts. These two factors alone resulted in a substantial economic impact on the whole region.

The famous Welsh singing festivals, which had been so popular, closed down during the revival because their famous vocalists, such as the "Sankeys" and "Alexanders" were now singing hymns in the revival meetings. The theaters and football stadiums likewise closed down for lack of interest. Political meetings were canceled or abandoned. Many of the elected officials, even those from London, abandoned their seats in parliament to participate in the revival meetings. Businesses founded upon honorable trades and products prospered. Those that traded on vice went out of business. Never before in history had an entire society been so profoundly transformed by a spiritual revival in such a short time.

THE CHURCH TRANSFORMED

The most significant result of this revival on the church was that seemingly all church prejudices and denominational barriers collapsed, as believers and pastors of all denominations began to worship the Lord together and gave themselves to gathering the great harvest. The quarrels of local Christians were either forgotten or instantly healed, with former offenses appearing petty and insignificant in the light of the Lord's glory.

One outstanding characteristic of the revival was the confession of sin, and it swelled over from the unsaved to the saved, who were all broken down and humbled by the revelation of the cross of Christ. Bitterness and resentment seemed unthinkable as all were compelled to gaze upon the Lord's great mercy and love. This brought forth a unity that was not caused by the fires of persecution, but by the presence of the Consuming Fire Himself, the glory and presence of the Lord. This was a historic example of how all of our individual crowns will be cast to the feet of the Lamb when He enters.

Churches that had struggled to keep the doors open for the few saints who would attend their services were now faced with the problem of how to accommodate the multitudes. Even the prayer meetings, which before would only draw a handful of faithful ones, were now overflowing, with people at times coming hours early just to get a seat. There was not a single congregation in Wales that was really prepared for the magnitude of this revival, but many of them learned fast how to cope with it. Some of the pastors strove to serve all of the new converts and see that they were properly incorporated into congregations, but the revival was from beginning to end "gloriously out of control."

Some of the pastors quickly burned out by trying to do too much. In fact, it is probable that the revival could have lasted longer and maybe even indefinitely if the leaders had taken care of themselves better. As Charles Finney once said, "No revival can last if the workers do not learn to rest." True revivals bring many strains upon congregations and Christian workers that few are prepared for. Almost every church or mission in the country grew dramatically, doubling or even quadrupling in membership in just the first days of the revival, and many maintained these members for years after the revival ended.

Even so, multitudes who were touched by the revival and had a genuine encounter with the Lord were also lost again to the world because there were not enough workers to help establish them on a strong foundation. It is hard to take the time to equip other workers and ministries in the heat of revival. Had this been done before the revival, many more of those who committed themselves to the Lord during this time could have been established in the faith and truly added to the church.

THE FIRE SPREADS

A true revival cannot be kept local. Revival is like a fire that is carried by the wind—its sparks will ignite the dry wood and grass in every direction that it blows. Sparks can be carried by letters, phone calls, or newspapers—but most of all they are carried by people. Localities that were far removed from the center of the Welsh Revival broke out into revival just at the news of what was happening in Wales. In many of these places, the awakening seemed to be just as intense as what was going on in Wales. The spiritual temperature of the entire world was raised a few degrees by this great outpouring of the Spirit.

On April 8, 1905, nearly ten thousand miles away in Los Angeles, California, a young man named Frank Bartleman heard F.B. Meyer preach, who had just come from Wales. As he described the revival that was going on in Wales and his meeting with Evan Roberts, Bartleman later wrote in his book, *Another Wave Of Revival* (page 8): "My soul was stirred to the depths, having read of this revival shortly before. I then and there promised God He should have full right of way with me; if He could use me."

Later Bartleman, William Seymour, and Pastor Smale of the First Baptist Church in Los Angeles read the book, *The Great Revival in Wales*, by S.B. Shaw, and G. Campbell Morgan's tract, *The Revival in Wales*, and were stirred to earnestly seek the Lord for revival in Los Angeles. In May, they were sent five thousand pamphlets titled *The Revival in Wales*, which they distributed in the churches. Bartleman wrote to Evan Roberts who wrote him back personally, with some instructions about how to prepare for revival. It was soon after this that the Azusa Street Revival erupted, and the great Pentecostal Movement was born. It would impact hundreds of millions of lives, and the fires from it continues to burn to this day.

Bartleman, Seymour, and Smale were unknowns ministering in a tiny little unknown mission on a side street in Los Angeles. Evan Roberts could not have known the impending spiritual destiny of these men without divine revelation. Because he took the time to communicate with such unknowns, history was changed and the last day course of the church was set on fire. These three great spiritual pioneers continually referred to their encouragement from Evan Roberts as they pursued the fullness of God's Spirit in their lives.

SPARKS FLY

The Welsh Revival had a powerful impact on many other unexpected places. Visiting preachers and ordinary believers who had come to see the "the burning bush," returned home to start fires in their own churches, mission fields, and cities. Christians all over the world were encouraged and emboldened by the news, and nothing ignites evangelism like encouragement in the church. When Christians are encouraged in their faith they cannot help but to share the hope that is within them. Only the Lord could know how many souls were birthed into the kingdom by the fires started in Wales. By that handful of young, zealous believers who yearned for Him, they opened the door for Him, and then followed Him.

The Welsh-speaking colonies in America and elsewhere were quickly set ablaze with revival. India was swept with the fire. All of Britain was touched and the continent was invaded by wave after wave of evangelists, pastors, Bible teachers, and even new believers who could not sit still with the good news that was burning inside of them. In Scandinavia, there are still hundreds of churches that trace their birth to the Welsh Revival. Rees Howells, the great intercessor, was among the young evangelists who carried the fire from Wales to the mission field. Waves of evangelists and missionaries swept across the continents of Africa and Asia, saving souls and planting churches, Bible schools, and colleges to the ends of the earth.

A young Latvian student from Spurgeon's College in London left his classes on hearing of the fire of God in Wales and headed for Swansea. There, the Spirit of God came upon him so mightily that when he returned to his native Russia, the revival broke out there. More than thirty years later, this man testified that he was still conscious of the effect of the Welsh revival upon his ministry, which directly resulted in tens of thousands coming to Christ and the planting of over two hundred churches in Eastern Europe. It is probable that similar testimonies could be given from men of God in almost every nation on earth. The fire was obviously centered in Wales, but the sparks were being carried everywhere to set the harvest fields ablaze.

Pastors D.P. and W.J. Williams, founders of the Apostolic Church in Europe, were both converted during the Welsh Revival. These men carried the fire of their conversions until their deaths. They impacted much of the church in Europe and started a worldwide movement devoted to returning apostolic church government to the church, which continues to this day.

It is impossible to speculate about what the twentieth century church would have been like without the extraordinary impact of the Welsh Revival. Though some denominations would not even acknowledge that the Welsh Revival was from God, it is probable that every church, movement, and denomination was influenced and changed to some degree by this mighty outpouring of God. But, as is the case with almost every true revival, it was the lowly and needy people who were touched the most. However, once touched they did not remain lowly and needy, but arose to embrace their destiny as the true royalty in the earth, sons and daughters of the King of kings. This brought great transformation not only to the church, but to society as a whole.

As stated, there probably has never been a revival that brought such a radical change upon society as a whole in such a short period of time as the great Welsh Revival. Even so, its greatest impact of all probably came through its influence on those who would be used to ignite the Azusa Street Revival, and the unprecedented impact on the modern church that it would have, though not in as short a period of time, but for over a century, and possibly even to the end of the age. This is where our story continues.

PART TWO
AZUSA

CHAPTER TWELVE
THE SEED

The strength and longevity of anything that is built will be affected by the strength of the foundation it is built upon. The church that is built upon the foundation of Jesus Christ will prevail forever just as He has. Any other foundation will ultimately fail. We must not even build upon the foundation of the Holy Spirit. He was sent to lead us to Jesus, and in all that we do we must be seeking Jesus. Even so, only the Holy Spirit can truly build the church upon the true foundation, and openness to Him in the work of the church is the most important element of true New Testament church life. Possibly the greatest contribution to this since the first century we owe to the great saints who led the revival at the old, broken down mission in a dirt poor neighborhood of Los Angeles—Azusa Street.

The Apostle Paul also warned that we must be careful how we build upon the foundation. He declared that all "wood, hay, stubble" (see I Corinthians 3:12 KJV) will be burned up and that only "gold, silver, and precious stones will remain." Therefore, in our studies of churches or movements we should look for things that have proven to be "wood, hay and stubble," which do not last, as well as those things which have proven to be "gold, silver and precious stones," which do last. The great apostle also promised that the fire would test the quality of every work. Revival fire is one of the ultimate tests, and Azusa ignited one of the most powerful, most enduring fires, in the nearly two thousand years of church history.

The beginning of the Pentecostal Movement is usually marked from the outpouring of the Holy Spirit at Azusa Street in 1906. There were a number of powerful ministries and movements which both experienced and promulgated the baptism of the Holy Spirit prior to Azusa Street, but none of them had the continuing impact that this one did. It was a true beginning, and it added something to the advancing church that has lasted. The movement has changed, and now has many different streams, but one can recognize what originated at Azusa as the source in most of the moves of God that have set the course of Christianity in the century since Azusa.

William J. Seymour and Frank Bartleman are the two names that are most often associated with the Azusa Street Revival. They were different in many ways, but they were both young men who had an uncommon desire to know the Lord and see His power restored to the church. Seymour was the unquestioned leader of the revival. He had the authority that gave birth to the movement on earth. Bartleman was the intercessor who seemed to have the authority in heaven.

Because these men were so different, their stories give us two very different views of the Azusa Street Revival. However, these different pictures do not conflict, but complement each other to give us a more complete picture. Though our main emphasis will be from Seymour's and Barlteman's perspectives, first we must go back a little further still.

THE GRANDFATHER OF AZUSA

Charles Fox Parham (1873-1929) presided over a Bible school in Topeka, Kansas. He was a true spiritual father, and many consider him the father of the modern Pentecostal Movement. Even though he would later reject many of his own spiritual children, his part in this movement must be recognized and understood.

Parham was a seeker of God who was constantly challenged by what he viewed as the great chasm between biblical Christianity and the then-present state of the church. He sought the Lord for what he considered to be a true, biblical expression of Christianity. As he was keeping a prayer vigil on New Year's Eve of the year 1900, he experienced the spiritual gift of "speaking in tongues," or "glossolalia," right after midnight on January 1, 1901, the precise dawning of the twentieth century. Few could have understood then how this one event would be used to define Christianity in the twentieth century.

Speaking in tongues or the use of other spiritual gifts is by no means unique in church history. Many reformers and revivalists had such experiences. Even so, Parham's experience came at what could be called "the fullness of time," or a time that was ripe for the harvest of a recovered truth. His experience created a huge interest, at least partly because of the dry and lifeless state of the church at the time. Also, Parham was not known for emotionalism or exaggeration, but rather the opposite. He was conservative and resolute, which at the time gave even more credibility to his experience.

A couple of years after his baptism in the Holy Spirit, Parham's health broke down and he was forced to move to Houston where he could stay with friends. His strength was recovered and he began another Bible school in the Texas port city. William Seymour became one of his students, but because he was black, and Parham was a strict segregationist, he had to sit outside of the classroom and listen through a door that Parham would leave cracked open for him.

Seymour wanted the Lord so much that he would embrace any humiliation to be close to what he felt that the Lord was doing. He was convinced that a new Pentecost was coming to the church, and that what Parham had experienced at the dawning of the century was prophetic of what was to come.

William J. Seymour was born in Centerville, Louisiana on May 2, 1870. He was the son of former slaves, Simon and Phyllis Seymour. After gaining their freedom, the Seymours continued working on a plantation. Young William followed in their footsteps, growing strong in body and spirit, but receiving little formal education. He taught himself to read so he could read the Bible.

Young William endured the nearly constant harassment of his race by the Ku Klux Klan and the humiliation of the oppressive Jim Crow laws. This caused Seymour to become convinced that Jesus Christ was the only true liberator of men. After contracting smallpox and losing one eye, he devoted himself to the ministry, proclaiming the Gospel of the true liberty to all men through Jesus Christ.

REJECTION MARKS THE SPOT

In January 1906, Seymour left Parham's school to pastor a mission congregation, without having received the baptism in the Holy Spirit that he had sought for so long. Just a week after arriving, he was rejected by congregational leaders of the mission who did not like his emphasis on the coming of a new Pentecost. Seymour was gracious and started a little prayer group of like-minded souls who simply had to experience more of God. They could not have been aware that when they did, the Christian world would be forever changed.

One recurring theme in church history seems to be that great leaders often arrive at their appointed place of destiny because of a rejection. We can see this also repeated in Scripture, such as in the lives of Joseph, Moses, David, and the Lord Jesus Himself, to name but a few. It seems as if a great disappointment with ourselves or men is a prerequisite to being used by God in a great way, especially to begin something new.

It could even be said that learning to deal with rejection by men comes on the list of instructions for being a Christian. We should never be surprised by it, but keep our trust and attention on the Lord who has promised to never leave or forsake us. He will also use every such thing that happens to us for His own good, as well as ours.

Long before Seymour made his way to Los Angeles, Frank Bartleman had been preparing the spiritual ground for what was coming. He was not a pastor, but a layman who loved the Lord and loved his city. He longed to see the Lord move in Los Angeles, and prayed for this continuously.

As we discussed previously, it was on April 8, 1904 that Frank Bartleman heard F.B. Meyer preach. Meyer was from London and had just returned from the Welsh Revival. Meyer was not a starter of revival fires, but he was a carrier. His descriptions of the revival in Wales would throw fuel on the flames of the flickering spiritual hope of all who heard him. After listening to Meyer, Frank Bartleman promised the Lord that He would have his full devotion from that time on. Many make such commitments in the heat of a moment, but Bartleman was a man of his word, and he kept his promise.

With his heart broken from the recent death of his three-year old daughter, Bartleman felt that his treasure was now in heaven, and he resolved to do everything for the sake of the Gospel. He began distributing tracts at the post office, banks, public buildings, saloons, and even houses of prostitution. He worked long and faithfully, but saw few lives changed. This caused him to yearn for more spiritual power. A great burden came upon him to see the kind of revival that he had heard about in Wales, which not only changed individuals, but changed cities. The more he worked, the more he travailed in heart for such a move of God to come to Los Angeles.

Then Bartleman began to sense that what was to come to Los Angeles would be different from what was happening in Wales. He began to boldly prophesy the coming of "another Pentecost." At this time, many other Christians around the world, seemingly independent of one another, were growing in an expectation of this gift of the Holy Spirit being poured out on the church again as it had in the first century. This was due to an emphasis on the biblical prophecies in both Joel 2 and Acts 2 that promised that this would happen in the last days. In this way the ground was actually being tilled for the fast spreading of this movement when the Holy Spirit came. In God's perfect timing, some of these people would come together in the little run-down mission in a converted stable on Azusa Street.

This is one of the unique elements to the Azusa Street Revival—it was not just centered on one man. Just as Barnabas had to go find Paul before he could be released into his own calling as an apostle, our own destinies are often dependent on our humility to seek out those with whom we need to be joined in His purposes. Even Jesus submitted Himself to the ministry of John the Baptist before proceeding with His own calling. The Lord has so composed His plan that we all need each other. The more we can humble ourselves to be joined to others, the more fruit we will ultimately bear.

On the first of May, a small revival broke out in the Lake Avenue Methodist Episcopal Church in Pasadena. Intercessors had been praying for a revival in Pasadena, and the Lord answered their prayers. Bartleman visited the church and was deeply touched. The altar was full of seeking souls, and it encouraged his resolve to see the Lord move that way in Los Angeles.

That night he made a prophetic notation in his journal. He began listing the future dangers that would surely try to sidetrack the coming revival he was convinced was near. He wrote that it would pass many churches by because they were satisfied, and that ultimate success or failure could depend on their staying humble enough to seek the grace of God. He felt that if those who were used in the revival became caught up with a sense of their own importance, this great spiritual opportunity would be lost. He wrote that:

> God has always sought a humble people. He can use no other... There is always much need for heart preparation, in humility and separation, before God can consistently come. The depth of any revival will be determined exactly by the spirit of repentance that is obtained. In fact, this is the key to every true revival born of God.

Bartleman then read the book, *The Great Revival in Wales*, by S.B. Shaw, and the fire in his heart could no longer be contained. He forsook his secular employment and devoted himself full-time to the ministry. He was at the point where he would either see revival or perish. He hungered so much for the move of God in the Spirit that he even lost his appetite for food. "Man shall not live by bread alone," he declared to those who were concerned for him. In his heart he had determined that it would be better to die than to miss the opportunity of a great move of God. He had so abandoned himself to God that he simply did not have any alternatives; he had nothing to fall back on in his life if God did not move. Such hunger, focus, and enduring devotion to the Lord would be set in the spiritual DNA of the Azusa Revival.

Bartleman began visiting with people all day long, giving them G. Campbell Morgan's pamphlet on the *Revival in Wales*. The pamphlet moved the hearts of many very deeply. Some were being enlisted to pray for a mighty outpouring of the Holy Spirit in the city. Bartleman was becoming so consumed with God that he began to wake up in the middle of the night shouting praises to Him. He wrote about this time:

> *I was now going day and night, exhorting myself to have faith in God for mighty things. The spirit of revival consumed me. The spirit of prophecy came upon me strongly also. I seemed to receive a definite "gift of faith" for revival. We were evidently in the beginning of wonderful days to come, and, I prophesied continually of a mighty outpouring.*

Bartleman's zeal for the Lord at this time was so great that his wife and friends began to fear for his life. He missed so much sleep and so many meals in order to pray that they did not think that he could last much longer. His response to their pleas for moderation was that he would rather die than not see revival.

Psalm 104:4 states that the Lord makes His messengers **"flames of fire."** This was the impartation that the Lord gave to the two men on the Road to Emmaus—hearts that burned for the message of the Son of God. Together, Bartleman and Seymour were such messengers. The fire that burned within them could not be quenched. Because of this they would be used to start possibly the greatest revival in history.

CHAPTER THIRTEEN

THE HEAT BUILDS

On June 17, Bartleman went to Los Angeles to attend a meeting at the First Baptist Church where they were waiting on God for the outpouring of His Spirit. Their pastor, Joseph Smale, had just returned from Wales. He was filled with zeal to have the same visitation and blessing come to his own church in Los Angeles, and was holding meetings every day and night to seek the Lord for His outpouring.

Often visiting Smale's church, Bartleman became discouraged by the fact that the people had to wait on the pastor to do anything. They would not even pray until he came. This stirred Bartleman to seek a deeper revelation of Jesus for himself. He would only sleep fitfully, often waking to pray and seek the Lord for hours at a time in the middle of the night. He yearned more than anything for a closer relationship with Him. He felt that the closer he became to the Lord, the harder it was on his flesh, but he did not care. He wanted to know **"the fellowship of His sufferings" (see Philippians 3:10),** the travail that the Lord felt for the lost. He began to experience what he later felt were the **". . .groanings that could not be uttered" (Romans 8:26 KJV).**

At a tent meeting, Bartleman met Edward Boehmer, who had just been converted the previous spring, but seemed to have the same burden of prayer on him. They were immediately united in spirit and seemed to feed each other's passion for revival. Bartleman later said, "My life was by this time literally swallowed up in prayer. I was praying day and night."

It was at this time that a concern began to arise in Bartleman for what he began to perceive to be an overemphasis on the Welsh Revival. It was news of that great revival that had first stirred his own heart, but he became uncomfortable with everyone praying for a revival like the one in Wales. He had started to sense that God wanted to do something different in Los Angeles, and he wanted the people to be open for it.

Even so, Bartleman then wrote a letter to Evan Roberts in Wales, asking him to pray for California. Roberts replied that he would, and this gave the church in Los Angeles their first link to the Welsh Revival leaders. Roberts exhorted them to: "Congregate the people together who are willing to make a total surrender. Pray and wait. Believe God's promises. Hold daily meetings." This letter was a great encouragement to Bartleman. The Spirit was now surely moving in California. Conviction was rapidly spreading among the people, and they were rallying from all over the city to the meetings at Pastor Smale's church.

Because of Bartleman's exhortations, the people had gradually allowed the Spirit to conduct the meetings and were not just looking to Pastor Smale. This devotion to the Spirit leading was in fact the model of the Welsh Revival and would be one of its great contributions to the church. Souls were now being saved all over the building, while the meeting swept on unguided by human hands. This caused the tide to rise rapidly, and sectarian barriers were being swept away by it.

Just as the disciples had gathered **"with one accord" (see Acts 2:1 NKJV)** on the Day of Pentecost when the Holy Spirit was first poured out, He always requires that the people be in unity before He moves in a great way. Now unity was coming to many in Los Angeles, and one could begin to sense the nearness of the match that was about to set the kindling on fire.

By this time meetings were not just running day and night, but often through the night. There was an almost uncontrollable passion for the Lord in the people, and it continued to spread. Pastor Smale also began to prophesy of wonderful things to come, including "the speedy return of the apostolic gifts to the church." People began to feel as if Los Angeles was a type of Jerusalem where the Spirit first came to dwell in men. By June 1906, the prayers had changed from praying for another revival like the one in Wales to praying for "another Pentecost."

On July 3, Bartleman and Boehmer were in a hall in Pasadena praying when the burden became almost unbearable for them. They cried out like a woman giving birth. When the burden finally lifted they just sat for awhile, enjoying the calm that seemed to envelop them. Suddenly the Lord Jesus revealed Himself, standing between them. They did not dare to move. Love swept over them and they felt as if a burning fire went through them. As Bartleman later wrote,

> ...my whole being seemed to flow down before Him, like wax before the fire. I lost all consciousness of time or space, being conscious only of His wonderful presence. I worshiped at His feet. It seemed a veritable Mount of Transfiguration. I was lost in the pure Spirit. The Lord had said nothing to us, but only overwhelmed our spirits by His presence. He had come to strengthen and assure us for His service. We knew now we were workers with Him, fellowshippers of His sufferings, in the ministry of "soul travail." Real soul travail is just as definite in the spirit as natural human birth-pangs. The simile is almost perfect in its sameness. No soul is ever born without this. All true revivals of salvation come this way.

It was at this time that Bartleman was reminded of what he felt was the keynote to revival: "The depth of revival will be determined exactly by the depth of the spirit of repentance. And this will hold true for all people, at all times."

The revival spirit at Pastor Smale's church was rapidly spreading over the city. Devoted intercessors came from all over the region representing almost all spiritual backgrounds. Soon they expanded their vision for just seeing a revival in Los Angeles to praying for the nation. Then they took another step of faith and began praying for a revival that would touch the ends of the earth. These prayers would be answered.

As Bartleman wrote in his journal at the time, "The spirit of prophecy began to work among us for mighty things on a large scale." While visiting Smale's church again, Bartleman was led to pray especially for faith, discernment of spirits, healing, and prophecy. When they had begun praying for revival a few months before, no one seemed to have much faith for anything out of the ordinary. There was skepticism in regard to the present condition of the church that cast itself like a pall over believers. With consistent intercession, this attitude changed. Now they had faith to not only pray for specific things, but for great things and to prophesy them.

It was then that Bartleman wrote an article for the *Daily News of Pasadena*, describing what he saw in Pastor Smale's church. When it was printed, the publisher was inspired to come out and see what was going on. He was greatly convicted, came to the altar, and sought God earnestly. He then wrote his own article that was copied in a number of Holiness papers throughout the country. It was entitled, "What I Saw in a Los Angeles Church." This began to create a nationwide interest in what was developing there.

After the meetings had run daily at the First Baptist Church for almost four months, the officials of the church were tired and wanted to return to the old order. Pastor Smale was told to either stop the revival or get out. He chose to leave. He then organized a New Testament Church, and Bartleman became a charter member, even though he expressed his dislike for such organization. He just went on preaching daily wherever he could find an audience and praying continually in-between.

CHAPTER FOURTEEN

THE DARK NIGHT OF THE SOUL

After several months at such an intense level, many began to faint and drift away. The spiritual heat that was building began to ebb. It was like the children of Israel leaving Egypt with such zeal, only to have it wither quickly in the wilderness they had to cross before getting to the Promised Land. The same thing had happened just before the outbreak of the Welsh Revival, as well as before the Day of Pentecost when the Spirit was first given to the church. Over five hundred had seen the resurrected Christ and were instructed to wait for the gift of the Holy Spirit in Jerusalem, but only one hundred twenty were left when the baptism came.

During this time the zeal did not wane in Bartleman. The burden for intercession so possessed him that he fasted and prayed almost continually. Neither his wife nor his friends could persuade him to stop, though they tried desperately, fearing that he could not survive much longer. Bartleman later said that he felt as if he were at

Gethsemane with the Lord. He even began to think that the travail of His soul had fallen upon him in such measure that he would not be able to see the answer to his prayers, and he would not be able to live that long under such intensity, but still he continued.

Some began to believe that Bartleman was losing his mind. Few could understand what he was going through. This was the apostolic intercession that compelled Paul to risk his life, to fast, pray, and give himself to "watchings" (all night prayer), to submit himself to beatings and stonings or anything else required for the sake of the Gospel. To the natural man these things are foolish, but they are the things of the Spirit, which the natural man cannot understand. Selfish people simply cannot understand sacrifice. Bartleman held to his faith that "he that would save his life shall lose it." **"Most assuredly, I say to you, unless a grain of wheat falls into the ground and dies, it remains alone; but *if it dies*, it produces much grain" (John 12:24 NKJV).** He did not care if he had to die; he needed revival more than he needed his present life.

The New Testament Church started by Brother Smale grew and began to take on so many secondary interests that they started to lose their interest in prayer. As they drifted from carrying the burden for revival, Bartleman likewise drifted away from them. Many start strong but do not endure long. Frank Bartleman was determined to pray until the fire of God fell, even if he had to do it alone.

As Bartleman continued his unyielding zeal for revival and prayer, and the New Testament Church drifted from these, opposition to him began to arise in the church. Some tried to get him to stop his prayer meetings. When Bartleman inquired of the Lord for His will, he had an encounter with the glory of the Lord. Without answering his questions directly, the Lord settled the matter. Bartleman was addicted to the presence of God and would rather do without air than prayer. "We ought to obey God rather than men" he declared when asked what he was going to do.

It was at that time when Bartleman wrote another article that fanned the sparks back into flames for many who had drifted from their hope for revival. In it he concluded with a prophecy that was soon to be fulfilled:

"Heroes will arise from the dust of obscure and despised circumstances, whose names will be emblazoned on heaven's eternal page of fame. The Spirit is brooding over our land again as at creation's dawn, and the decree of God goes forth—'Let there be light!' Brother, sister, if we all believed God, can you realize what would happen? Many of us here are living for nothing else. A volume of believing prayer is ascending to the throne night and day. Los Angeles, Southern California, and the whole continent shall surely find itself before long in the throes of a mighty revival, by the Spirit and power of God" (Way of Faith, Nov. 16, 1905).

After a service in the New Testament Church, Bartleman and a few others were led to begin praying for the Lord to pour out His Spirit speedily, "with signs following." They did not have "tongues" in mind, and later asserted that at the time they had not even heard or thought of such a thing. This was in February 1906.

On March 26, Bartleman went to a cottage meeting on Bonnie Brae Street. Both white and black believers were meeting there for prayer. He had just met William Seymour, who had recently come from Texas. Of that meeting he recorded in his journal a simple note about Seymour: "He was a black man, blind in one eye, very plain, spiritual, and humble. He attended the meetings at Bonnie Brae Street."

When Bartleman met Seymour, it marked the beginning of the dawn after his dark night of the soul. Both men lived and breathed a passion for revival, and especially "another Pentecost." It is unlikely that they ever even sat down to discuss how they would work together, but it is obvious that the Azusa Street Revival would not have been possible without either one of them. One was nitro and the other was glycerin. Alone neither was accomplishing much; together they created an explosion that rocked the entire Christian world.

The Lord still sends His disciples out two by two. Regardless of who we are and what the Lord has entrusted to us, we will not be able to accomplish what we have been called to do without others. Like the meeting of Paul and Barnabas, the meeting of Seymour and Bartleman marks one of the great demarcation points in the history of Christianity.

CHAPTER FIFTEEN

THE FIRE FALLS AT AZUSA

Seymour had recognized the hand of God in his rejection by the mission and was content serving the little home prayer group, which met regularly for several months. Seymour's hope was not on the appearance of things on the earth, but on what God would send from heaven. While in the middle of a ten-day fast, Seymour and the others in this little band were dramatically baptized in the Holy Spirit, receiving the gift of tongues as well as other spiritual gifts.

As stated, this was not unique in history, but never before had this experience itself become an actual movement. This time it did. Word spread "like fire in a dry wood" and like the first Pentecost, multitudes came to see what had happened at Seymour's prayer group. This interest had obviously been fueled by Frank Bartleman's stream of articles, tracts, and faithful ministry throughout the city, exhorting churches and prayer groups to seek the Lord for "a new Pentecost."

As soon as word was out about the experience that came upon Seymour's prayer group, large crowds of interested people descended on them. To accommodate the hungry people, they were forced to rent a run-down old barn-like building in the middle of a black ghetto. At the time, no one imagined that the little street that it was on, Azusa, would soon be called "the most famous address in the world."

The former mission had a dirt floor and was once used as a livery stable. Many remarked when they came that the Lord Himself had been born in just such a place. The rent was only eight dollars a month, and it could hold as many as nine hundred people. Even so, services were soon going almost around the clock to handle the crowds that were coming.

What had begun as a spark with Charles Parham now leapt into open flames. It would capture the attention of millions around the world and quickly spread to every recognized nation on earth. A humble little prayer group, led by a one-eyed former sharecropper, was the seedbed for the dawning of a new age in Christianity.

On Sunday morning, April 15, a black sister from the Bonnie Brae meeting attended the service at New Testament Church and spoke in tongues. It created a great stir. Almost like the first Day of Pentecost, the people gathered in little companies on the sidewalk after the service inquiring about what was happening, and what it meant.

The little group at Bonnie Brae had been tarrying earnestly for an outpouring of the Holy Spirit. In April the Spirit had come in a similar manner to the original Day of Pentecost. When Bartleman heard of it that Sunday morning, he went to Bonnie Brae immediately. He later wrote of that day:

We had been praying for many months for victory. Jesus was now "showing Himself alive" again to many. The pioneers had broken through for the multitude to follow.

There was a general spirit of humility manifested in the meeting. They were taken up with God. Evidently the Lord had found the little company at last, outside as always, through whom He could have His way. God had not chosen an established mission where this could be done. They were in the hands of men; the Spirit could not work. Others far more pretentious had failed. That which man esteems had been passed by once more, and the Spirit born again in a humble "stable" outside ecclesiastical establishments.

A body must be prepared, in repentance and humility, for every outpouring of the Spirit. The preaching of the Reformation was begun by Martin Luther in a tumble down building in the midst of the public square in Wittenberg. D'Aubigne describes it as follows: "In the middle of the square at Wittenberg stood an ancient wooden chapel, thirty feet long and twenty feet wide, whose walls, propped up on all sides, were falling into ruin. An old pulpit made of planks, and three feet high, received the preacher. It was in this wretched place that the preaching of the Reformation began. It was God's will that which

*was to restore His glory should have the humblest
surroundings. It was in this wretched enclosure that
God willed, so to speak, that His well-beloved Son
should be born a second time. Among those thousands
of cathedrals and parish churches with which the
world is filled, there was not one at that time which
God chose for the glorious preaching of eternal life."*

Like most of the great moves of God in history, when
the great Pentecostal revival began, very few understood
the true significance of what was happening, even those
who had been used to prophesy its coming. It did not start
as a large mass movement, but as a little prayer meeting.
That is a part of the wonder and awe of being a Christian.

When we are relating to Almighty God, the One who
created the world with a word, anything that He decides
to breathe upon can have consequences far beyond any
human comprehension. Because He is God, He can take
the most humble prayer meeting and use it to shake the
world. Because He delights in using the humble, the weak,
and even the foolish, a simple meeting can have historic
consequences. For this reason, we should never doubt the
potential of even the most humble gathering of those who
know Him. Whenever two or more gather, He will be
there. If just two can agree together, anything is possible.

The Lord does usually do great things after a time of
preparation. He uses men and women who, like Frank
Bartleman, have such a passion for the Lord and His
purposes that they impart it to others. When the fire
is finally lit, it can then jump all humanly imposed
boundaries and move beyond human control.

Every great spiritual pioneer who has been used to ignite great moves of God has, at least at first, appeared reckless and dangerous to the church they were sent to awaken. Seymour and Bartleman were no exceptions to this. They wanted God so much that they did not care what anyone else thought about it. They could not live within the present limits of their time, so they were used to push those limits back. Their abandonment to the Spirit was then used to benefit multiplied millions who would follow.

From the beginning, Azusa broke many norms to the degree that it was astonishingly unique. Even in the first meetings, the seeds of the great movements birthed out of it can be seen. Following is Bartleman's own description of his first visits to the little mission on Azusa Street:

After a season of prayer, I was impressed of the Lord to go to the meeting, which had been removed from Bonnie Brae Street to 312 Azusa Street. Here they had rented an old frame building, formerly a Methodist church, in the center of the city but now a long time out of use for meetings. It had become a receptacle for old lumber, plaster, etc. They had cleared space enough in the surrounding dirt and debris to lay some planks on top of empty nail kegs, with seats enough for possibly thirty people. If I remember rightly, these were arranged in a square facing one another.

I was under tremendous pressure to get to the meeting that evening. It was my first visit to Azusa Mission. Mother Wheaton, who was living with us, was going with me. She was so slow that I could hardly wait for her. We finally reached Azusa and found about a dozen saints there, some white, some black. Brother Seymour was in charge. The "Ark of God" moved off slowly, but surely, at Azusa. It was carried on the shoulders of His own appointed priests in the beginning. We had no "new cart" in those days to please the carnal, mixed multitude. We had the devil to fight, but the Ark was not drawn by oxen (dumb beasts). The priests were "alive unto God," through much preparation and prayer.

Discernment was not perfect, and the enemy got some advantage which brought reproach to the work, but the saints soon learned to "take the precious from the vile." The combined forces of hell were set determinedly against us in the beginning. It was not all blessing. In fact, the fight was terrific. As always, the devil combed the country for crooked spirits to destroy the work if possible. But the fire could not be smothered. Gradually the tide arose in victory. But from a small beginning, a very little flame.

It was soon noised abroad that God was working at Azusa, and all kinds of people began to come to the meetings. Many were curious and unbelieving, but others were hungry for God. The newspapers began to ridicule and abuse the meetings, thus giving us much free advertising. This brought the crowds. The devil overdid himself again. Outside persecution never hurt the work. We had the most to fear from the working of evil spirits within. Even spiritualists and *hypnotists came to investigate, and to try their influence. Then all the religious soreheads, crooks and cranks came, seeking a place in the work. We had the most to fear from these. But this is always the danger to every new work; they had no place elsewhere. This condition cast a fear over many which was hard to overcome. It hindered the Spirit much. Many were afraid to seek God for fear the devil might get them.*

We found early in the Azusa work that when we attempted to steady the Ark, the Lord stopped working. We dared not call the attention of the people too much to the working of the evil one. Fear would follow. We could only pray and then God would give us victory. There was a presence of God with us, through prayer, we could depend on. The leaders had limited experience, and the wonder is that the work survived at all against its powerful adversaries. But it was of God. That was the secret.

A certain writer has well said: "On the day of Pentecost, Christianity faced the world, a new religion without a college, a people, or a patron. All that was ancient and venerable rose up before her in solid opposition, and she did not flatter or conciliate any one of them. She assailed every existing system and every bad habit, burning her way through innumerable forms of opposition. This she accomplished with her 'tongue of fire' alone."

Another writer has said: "The apostasy of the early Church came as a result of a greater desire to see the spread of its power and rule than to see new natures given to its individual members. The moment we covet a large following and rejoice in the crowd that is attracted by our presentation of what we consider truth, and have not a greater desire to see the natures of individuals changed according to the divine plan, we start to travel the same road of apostasy. . ."

The leaders of the Azusa work were inexperienced in leadership, but well-seasoned in faith. They trusted God to make up their lack, and for as long as they maintained that humility, He did make up for all the human weaknesses. It survived every onslaught of the devil and the religiously deceived. Missionaries and Christian leaders came from the far corners of the earth, and God touched all who came as sincere seekers of His grace.

THE BIRTH OF MODERN PENTECOSTAL MISSIONS

One of the great spiritual pioneers of the twentieth century, Dr. A.G. Garr, closed his ministry at the Burning Bush Hall to go to Azusa. He was reportedly the first white man to receive the baptism in the Spirit, and he quickly departed for North Carolina to hold revival meetings and pray for the release of the Holy Spirit there. He then went on to India, and then China to spread the fire, making him the first modern Pentecostal missionary. Through Dr. Garr hundreds of missionaries in the field received the baptism. Within a year, the fires of Pentecost were burning around the world.

Dr. Garr later returned to Charlotte, North Carolina, and became one of the remarkable spiritual pioneers of the time. He was the first to use tents for revivals, skits for street outreaches, and even produced the first Christian television program. He emphasized the Lord's love for healing to the degree that for the entire time that he was the pastor of the Pentecostal congregation in Charlotte, North Carolina, no one in his church needed a doctor.

Brother Smale came to Azusa to look up his members, many of which had left to be a part of the new move of God. He invited them back, promising them liberty in the Spirit. Many returned, and for a time the Lord moved mightily at the New Testament Church, also.

A.S. Worrell, translator of the New Testament, visited Azusa and declared that the work there had "rediscovered the blood of Christ for the Church at that time." Great emphasis was placed on the blood of Christ, and a high standard "for a clean life" was raised from the very beginning.

There was also a devotion to allowing the Holy Spirit to oversee the meetings. When presumptuous men would try to use the meetings for their own platform, strange things would happen to them. Some would lose their breath so that they could not speak. Others would forget what they wanted to say and sit down. Some even went blind for a time. According to Bartleman, no one got away with presumption in the early meetings.

It was often said of the revival at Azusa, just as it was written of the first century church, that the people experienced continual awe and wonder at the great things that God was doing. Every day was set on fire with the great acts of God. There was a great interest and focus on the Holy Spirit and spiritual gifts, but by far the main emphasis of the revival was knowing God and getting closer to Him. He was among them in such a tangible way that day and night He was in their hearts and minds. They simply loved God and sought Him like few others have before or since.

CHAPTER SIXTEEN

MAKING DISCIPLES OF ALL NATIONS

A remarkable characteristic of this revival from the beginning was the diversity of the people who were drawn to it. Some considered it unprecedented since the Day of Pentecost when men from every nation had gathered in Jerusalem. Even a prominent Jewish Rabbi in Los Angeles announced his full support of the revival. Soon remarkable healing miracles and dramatic conversions were taking place almost daily.

The church at the time was so dry that each testimony was like sparks in a dry wood—flames would ignite very fast. Newspaper articles fanned the flames into greater intensity. Testimonies from the Welsh Revival had stirred thousands to seek the Lord for revival in America, and the deplorable spiritual state of the country made her ready for it. Because of this, the fire spread faster than possibly any previous or subsequent revival in American history.

Seymour started a little paper to teach about the renewal to try and answer questions. He printed five thousand copies, which were passed around until they fell apart. Soon he was printing fifty thousand, but he still could not keep up with the demand.

Within weeks, a steady stream of missionaries was coming from every continent. Missionaries, who were on the front lines of the battle against the forces of darkness, were the most acutely aware of the fact that they needed more power. Just as the Lord told His disciples that they would receive power to be His witnesses when the Holy Spirit came upon them (see Acts 1:8), this same baptism had become the only hope for effective ministry that many of the missionaries now had. They came as desperate seekers and left filled with the power they had been seeking. Within months, Gospel fires were burning all over the world. In just two years the movement had taken root in over fifty nations, and was thought to have penetrated every United States town with a population of more than three thousand.

Because missionaries were some of the first to come, missions remain a fundamental part of the spiritual genetic code of the Pentecostal Movement and are one of its greatest strengths to this day. Throughout the Scriptures, it is seen that the power of God has always come in its greatest demonstrations where there was the greatest darkness. The first ones to carry the Pentecostal Movement abroad were seasoned missionaries who used the power they had been given. Multitudes of men, women, and children were delivered from bondage by these newly empowered missionaries. Those who were delivered went forth to deliver others. Soon missionary reports sent back to home churches read like a modern Book of Acts, adding even more fuel to the fire of the movement at home.

The Apostle Paul lamented that there were many teachers but not many fathers (see I Corinthians 4:15). A spiritual father does more than just teach—he reproduces what he has received in others. There was an essence to the Pentecostal Revival from the beginning that compelled everyone to not be content to just learn about the Lord, but to know Him through personal experience. People were taught not just to be spectators, but to demonstrate. When it was learned that the greatest demonstrations of the Spirit's power usually came in the darkest, neediest places, it compelled many to go on mission trips just to witness the power of God. This added great strength and depth to the new movement, touching the entire church with the needs of the nations, which kept it growing throughout the world as well as at home.

SPIRITUAL FATHERS EMERGE

Pentecostal children grew up constantly hearing the testimonies of God's power from missionaries. Because such esteem was given to these missionaries, they often became the children's greatest heroes. Emulating their heroes, many of these children of the early Pentecostal pioneers grew up to be missionaries so that they could live closest to such wonderful activities of the Spirit.

Others became pastors and evangelists who founded new churches and ministries all across the world. Many of these are now leaders of the great Pentecostal churches and denominations. Each of them is like a vast treasure house filled with experiences and stories of the glory of God. They walked with Him and learned His ways. They learned to be hosts to the Holy Spirit. They grew up believing that the Book of Acts was not just a history book, but a living guide for normal church life. Many of their own stories read like a modern Book of Acts as they earned their place as elders of the church.

We do not see in order to believe, but we believe in order to see. Because it is basic Pentecostal theology that God is the same today as He was yesterday and that He does everything today that He did in Scripture, true Pentecostals believe in His present working, and so they see it. Many Pentecostals will begin to wonder where they have gone wrong if they are not witnessing regular demonstrations of the power of God. To them, it is blasphemy to think that God was an author who wrote just one book and then retired. They must have a living relationship with a living God, and so they do see Him and His great works.

This was the experience at Azusa Street. Believers were in constant awe at the works of God in their midst. People forgot to eat or sleep, sometimes for days at a time, because they were so caught up in the presence of the Lord. Many claimed that they were simply afraid if they slept, they would miss something. Like the manna that came from heaven, every day they expected a fresh experience with the Lord. Faith built on faith until the humble little mission really had become a window of heaven.

At any given time, the Azusa Mission would be packed with such a diversity of people that some considered this almost as much of a marvel as the extraordinary miracles that were taking place. It began with a few black men and women in a little prayer group, but soon most of those who came were white. In one meeting, more than twenty nationalities were counted. Fine ladies could be found lying prostrate on the floor next to domestic servants and washerwomen. Prominent churchmen and high government officials sat next to hobos. No one seemed to care. They all had one thing in common—they came to see and experience God and be filled with His Holy Spirit.

Those who were baptized by the Holy Spirit started to see each other through the eyes of the Holy Spirit, not just after the flesh, or outward appearances. The more we are able to see by the eyes of the Spirit, the closer we will come to the Lord's ultimate purpose for His church—to be a house of prayer for all nations. Somehow the gift of tongues, which was a primary evidence of this revival helped people, who were otherwise very different, accept one another in the Lord. Later, this one gift would be used as a point of division within the church, but it was not that way in the beginning.

THE GREATEST MIRACLE

At the height of the Azusa Street revival, Seymour prophesied, "We are on the verge of the greatest miracle the world has ever seen." The miracle he was referring to was what we have already said a lot about—a true love and unity between races and creeds that he considered to be fundamental Christianity. He did not live to see the completion of his dream, but he fully expected the renewal to ultimately accomplish it.

As the movement has continued in a number of different forms, it is still more than possible; it is inevitable that his dream will come true. When it does, William J. Seymour must be considered as one who sowed the seeds for this greatest miracle of all. Possibly more than any other man in church history, he promoted that which alone can bring it to pass, seeking the fullness of the Holy Spirit in our midst. If we are truly filled with the Spirit we will not just see and know each other after the flesh or after the externals, but we will start to see each other as the Spirit does, and we will be one.

Above all things, the Holy Spirit has come to testify of Jesus. He alone can truly convict us of our sins and lead us into all truth. When the Holy Spirit manifests Himself in our midst, we will not see the world in shades of black and white; we will only see the glory of the Son of God. He has been given to help us see as God sees. God does not look on the outward appearance, but on the heart. God does not just see us as we are now, but He sees us through the blood of His Son and as we are to become—made in the likeness of Jesus. We must begin to see each other the same way. Racism is one of the ultimate evil strongholds in the human heart, and a sure evidence of the grip of evil. Likewise, true spiritual maturity will always result in unity and in the Lord's house truly becoming **"a house of prayer for all the nations,"** **(see Mark 11:17)** or as this reads literally, "a house of prayer for all ethnic groups."

Paul the Apostle had said that **"tongues are for a sign. . ." (I Corinthians 14:22),** and that sign seemed to have been given on the first Day of Pentecost. That day men from every nation heard the glories of God in their own languages. This was the first time since the Tower of Babel and the scattering of men's languages that this had happened. The sign was that the church would be the antithesis of the Tower of Babel, where men were scattered from each other. In the church, we will all be re-gathered as one.

Even as fractured and divided as the Pentecostal Movement may presently be, it has the destiny and calling to help bring unity to the whole church. This fire still burns in the Pentecostal Movement. Though it may now seem to be but a flicker, it will ignite again into a mighty blaze that will burn until all of the wood, hay, and stubble has been consumed, and the gold, silver and precious stones have been purified. Each movement may be fashioned into a different stone, but the day is coming when we will all be fashioned together into one crown of glory.

The explosive spread of the movement that began at Azusa, continued as long as the Holy Spirit was free to move as He willed, and the people sat before Him as one. As the revival drifted from these basics, they also drifted from the Source of their power. Where the Spirit of the Lord is, there must be liberty, and where He is Lord there will be unity. Before the Lord we all look the same. The blood of Jesus does wash away all color lines.

It is interesting to note that the very name Azusa was derived from an Indian word that means "blessed miracle." This was first noted by Father Juan Crespi in 1769, while on the Portola expedition to explore California. At that time, Azusa referred to the site of an old Indian village south of present-day Los Angeles in the San Gabriel Canyon. There a young Indian girl named Coma Lee prayed and fasted for the healing of her people. She was gifted with healing power as she laid hands on the sick. After she prayed for a chief who was wonderfully healed, he gave her the name Azusa to commemorate his miracle of healing. For many years, Azusa continued her healing ministry while her fame spread all over Southern California. During that time whenever there was suffering, people said, "Go to Azusa and be healed. . .go to Azusa." Maybe it is time for us to again go to Azusa and be healed.

CHAPTER SEVENTEEN

DEFEATED BY A SECONDARY SUCCESS

It seems that the Lord had ordained Pastor Smale to be the one to ignite the great Pentecostal outpouring of the twentieth century. He could have had this honor for eternity, but he was not so used because he tripped over the stumbling block that has stopped countless others from achieving their destinies. His local congregation became so successful that he lost his bigger vision. As Woodrow Wilson once said, "A man may be defeated by his own secondary successes."

This is not to in any way belittle the importance of building our local churches. They are the front line of what God is doing in the earth, they are the primary work of God in this age, and they need to be a primary focus of Christian leaders. However, when one is called to a larger purpose, as Smale was, good can be the worst enemy of best. Where would the church be today if Paul had rejected the apostolic call so that he could stay to build up the local church at Antioch? We would probably be in the same place because God would have used someone else, but it is likely that we would have never heard of Paul.

Smale became a respected pastor of a nice little church, but he could have been used to spark one of the greatest moves of God of all time. That honor now belongs to William J. Seymour, a humble black man who loved God more than any human honors or earthly riches. Seymour began the movement that would shake the world and redefine modern Christianity. In heaven, Seymour is certainly named with the great reformers and heroes of the church age.

Bartleman was gracious in his analysis of what transpired when Smale rejected the call to go on, saying: "God found His Moses in the person of Brother Smale to lead us to the Jordan crossing. But He chose Brother Seymour for our Joshua, to lead us over." Bartleman stayed with the mission for a long time before he received the baptism himself. After his baptism, he had an encounter with the Lord that would direct him for the rest of his life. The following is his own description of this encounter:

After God filled me, His Spirit rested mightily upon me one morning, and He said to me: "If you were only small enough, I could do anything with you." A great desire to be little, yea, to be nothing, came into my heart. But it has been oh so hard to keep low enough for Him to really work through me. And He only really uses me when I am little in my own eyes and really humble at His feet.

The fact is when a man gets to the place where he really loves obscurity, where he does not care to preach, and where he would rather sit in the back seat than on the platform, then God can lift him up and use him, and not very much before.

This seemed to be a summation of a primary message of God through Azusa. As long as the people were willing to be obscure, not jockeying for position or recognition, the fire not only continued to burn, but continued to increase. As soon as self-seeking, self-promotion, or even self-preservation enters, where we become more focused on protecting what we have than in seeking more of God, the end is near.

These things brought an end to the little mission on Azusa Street. It would move on to other places, and did become one of the greatest moves of God in history. Seymour was used mightily to begin the revival and lead it through its most fragile times, but then he, too, succumbed to the temptation to exalt the lesser purposes above the higher one.

For many months, the little mission was filled with the glory. Awe and wonder at the great things that God was doing permeated every meeting. The larger and more popular the movement became, the more the destroyer of revivals crept in, *the control spirit.*

Bartleman issued a prophetic warning that the grace of God would be lifted if they tried to organize the move of the Holy Spirit. He exhorted them that the Lord had to be free and that the true Pentecost could not become a sectarian barrier, but must remain available to all people. "To try to formulate a separate body is but to advertise our failure," he concluded.

The very next day, as they came to the meeting, there was a sign hanging on the building, which read "Apostolic Faith Mission." He knew then that the beginning of the end had come for that little mission, and he was right. From that time, the trouble and division began. Controversy is to be expected with every move of God, and when rivalry between the mission and other churches arose, the end was certainly near. The grace of the Holy Spirit to subdue the presumptuous was lifted, and contention entered the meetings. Strange doctrines started to come forth and bring more reproach.

In the beginning, the Spirit's work was so deep, and the people so hungry for God alone, that any time a carnal, human spirit was injected into the meetings it was discerned easily, as if a stranger had broken in through a window. Now open fanaticism went unchecked. The handwriting was on the wall. The glory quickly departed.

By the end of 1907, it seemed that a control spirit had taken the place of the Holy Spirit, not just at Azusa, but at many of the other Pentecostal meetings in the city as well. There was little discernable love between the brethren, and a lot of jealousy. Fights between the Pentecostals became increasingly vicious. That was the final affront to the presence of the Holy Spirit at Azusa, and He departed. The Pillar of Fire moved and grew into possibly the greatest move of God in church history, but the mission at Azusa faded into obscurity and then died altogether.

Today, there is a parking lot where the little mission stood, and even though this great revival died in seeming infamy, we can be sure that in heaven there is a monument to the great souls who wanted God so much that they were willing to press beyond the limits of their time and touch the possibilities of eternity at Azusa Street.

CHAPTER EIGHTEEN
THE GATES OF HELL SHALL NOT PREVAIL

I t is a well-known proverb that, "Those who do not know history are doomed to repeat it." Almost all of the great revivals in history died in some kind of infamy. Even though Jesus Himself affirmed that every time the Lord sows wheat the enemy will come along and sow tares in the same field (see Matthew 13:24-30), it is obviously not God's will for any revival or movement to end the way most of them do. The enemy has been able to sidetrack almost every one using the very same tactics, and they are still seldom discerned. We need to honor the great leaders whose spiritual hunger and spiritual sensitivity enabled something as extraordinary as Azusa Street to happen in the first place. But we also need to examine some of the things that obviously went wrong at Azusa Street—not for the purpose of criticism, but if possible to avoid doing the same things if God desires to use us in a great way.

One of the most devastating attacks upon the work of Azusa came when Charles Parham visited Seymour, his former student, in the fall of 1906. He wanted to see for himself the great work that had so quickly become the talk of Christians around the world. Seymour was thrilled by the visit from his mentor, warmly welcoming him with great honor and fanfare. However, Parham was deeply offended by what he saw. He thought that the various charismatic gifts were too openly demonstrated, and he was appalled by the way so many fell to the ground in apparent trances (one report described Azusa as sometimes resembling "a forest of fallen trees").

Seymour did realize that some were faking the manifestations, and he believed that these were tares sent by the devil to foul the field of wheat. Even so, he held to the biblical wisdom of letting the wheat and tares grow up together. He knew that if he tried to root out the tares, the wheat would also be uprooted. He responded to Parham that if he stopped that which was not real, he would also quench the Spirit and the work that was real. He determined that the risk of having some problems was acceptable in view of the spiritual benefits. When he later succumbed to the pressure and changed this policy, the revival at the Azusa Street Mission quickly died, and the revival was carried on through others in other places.

Even more than the faking of experiences, Parham was appalled by the unusual social and racial integration. Parham admired the Ku Klux Klan, and he especially objected to racial mixing or mingling during worship and at the altar. However, he did not believe this out of racial pride, but because of a false doctrine. He believed the great sin of humanity, which caused the judgment of the flood was racial mixing, and that Noah was chosen to survive because of his pedigree, being "without mixed blood." This is a tragic misunderstanding of Scripture that has been the twisted theological basis upon which many racist groups, including the Nazis, have been built.

The Bible does say that Noah was chosen because he was **"perfect in his generations"** (see **Genesis 6:9** KJV), or literally, "perfect in his genealogy," but this had nothing to do with the mixing of human races. The mixture that so offended the Lord was the mixture of the fallen angels with men, which had produced the superhuman **"nephilim"** (see **Genesis 6:4**). This was a race that the Lord did not create and they threatened the destruction of men whom He did create and also planned to redeem. This seems to have been Satan's attempt to pre-empt the "new creation" that would be brought forth when the Lord gave His Spirit to men.

In contrast to Parham's philosophy, Seymour felt that an essential element of Christianity itself was a unity which saw beyond the barriers of race, color, gender, nationality, class, or status. This was a demonstration that God is no respecter of persons and that all believers are truly one in Christ. To him, the Azusa Street Mission was becoming a taste of what true Christianity was meant to be, just as the first Pentecost saw the coming together of those from every nation.

Seymour's leadership of such a renewal marked by interracial equality, harmony, and unity, is even more remarkable when it is understood that this took place during the most severely segregated time in American history. It was also composed mostly of the two most embittered racial groups—the poor whites and poor blacks. When the revival spread, it was also most readily received in the Southern states where this racial conflict was then most prevalent. This is a sign of true revival. Just as water always flows to the lowest place, the waters of God always flow to the lowest points, and He sends His light to the darkest places. The true light of the Gospel, the essence of Christianity, has no place for racism, one of the ultimate demonstrations of pride, which God promises to resist.

Concerning the Azusa Street Revival, a leading British clergyman, A.A. Boddy, wrote, "One of the most remarkable things [about the revival] was that preachers of the Southern states were willing and eager to go over to those Negro people in Los Angeles and have fellowship with them." Frank Bartleman wrote, "The color line was washed away in the blood."

Charles Parham had been mightily used by God at times, but the seeds of deception from some of his doctrines were maturing at a time when the enemy could make the greatest use of them. This has been a tragic way in which history has continually repeated itself. Those who begin a movement will almost always persecute those who seek to take it further, or who are used to start another subsequent movement.

One of the worst curses placed upon biblical Israelites for their apostasy was that they would eat their own children. The apostasy of the church has brought this terrible curse upon itself as well, in almost every generation. Tragically, spiritual fathers seem to inevitably try to devour their own spiritual children just as Parham ultimately did.

When Parham could not force his style of leadership upon the Azusa Street Mission, he denounced it and started another rival mission at the fashionable Women's Christian Temperance Union Building. This was the first schism in the Pentecostal Movement. This man who could have had such a place of honor was used to sow the tares of racism and division into the Pentecostal Movement. When this rival mission started by Parham failed, he spent the rest of his life denouncing Seymour and the Azusa Street Revival. By this, he sealed the doom of his own ministry. He continually lost influence and followers until his death in 1929.

The tares of racism and division that Parham sowed into the work at Azusa remain in many parts of the Pentecostal Movement to this day. It was in this same fashion that the great reformer, Martin Luther, who was used to so dramatically change the church and the world for good, also sowed the seeds of racism, especially in relation to the Jewish people, doctrines which many believe to have been the foundation of the Nazi persecution of the Jews.

In this sad part of the story, we can see how the enemy will often use spiritual fathers and leaders who become "old wineskins," rigid and inflexible, to assault a new movement. This is one of the most powerful weapons of the enemy, whose most powerful guise is as "the accuser of the brethren." One of the most powerful forces at work in the Azusa Street Revival was its racial and national diversity, so this is what Satan used as his biggest weapon of attack.

Sadly, we can still expect Satan's biggest attacks against new movements to come through spiritual fathers or grandfathers who lose their control over the newer emerging movements. These will usually be directed at what are the strongest elements of the new movements. Obviously, the Lord could stop this, but He allows it for the purification of those who sincerely love the truth.

The Pentecostal/Charismatic Movement began under the leadership of a black man and with a small group of black people. They freely shared what they had been given, and were delighted when they saw the Spirit poured out on those from other races, especially whites. They felt that the Lord had given them the greatest gift, and they were thrilled that they were able to share it with their white brethren. That this great worldwide revival was a contribution from the black community has never been denied by white Pentecostals, but it is often forgotten.

Many of the white leaders who themselves went to Azusa Street to receive the baptism, remarkably still held to the prevalent segregationist beliefs of the time. They took the blessing back home to their all-white congregations in which no blacks were welcome. This was not true of all, but it was of most, and the entire

Pentecostal Movement quickly developed into the white and black streams that still prevail today.

However, the separate black and white streams in this movement were not the way it began, and it obviously was not the way that the Lord wanted it. The spiritual battle that began to rage against the baptism in the Holy Spirit itself was probably the most fierce persecution that Christians had experienced at the hands of other Christians in centuries.

Until the Charismatic Renewal made speaking in tongues almost fashionable, the price for being a Pentecostal was very high, and those early Pentecostal pioneers must be considered some of the great heroes of the faith. Caricatures of Pentecostals were carried in newspapers across the country, depicting them as anything from devil worshipers to lunatics. Employment was difficult, if not impossible, for anyone found out to be a Pentecostal. The houses and the church buildings of Pentecostals were often burned, and their children were ostracized, called "devil worshipers," and subjected to ruthless beatings by other children. Many had to flee from the homes and towns that they had grown up in.

Both the press and historians have turned a blind eye to this persecution against Pentecostals. It was, at times, as terrible and degrading as what African-Americans suffered under segregation. For black Pentecostals, it was a double jeopardy, as they were secluded from the white culture because of their race, and then from the black culture because of their religion. Just as the first Reformers risked all that they had so that later generations could enjoy religious freedom, two generations of Pentecostals paid the price for our freedom to know the Holy Spirit in our churches the way that we do today. They did it because they loved the Holy Spirit, and they counted knowing Him and allowing Him freedom in the church as more important than any freedom that the world could give them.

Those who paid this great price for our freedom are worthy of great honor, even if they did not get everything right. It was their sacrifices that made possible the truth and liberty in the Holy Spirit that so many Christians enjoy today. For this reason William Seymour is, and should be, considered one of the great Christian leaders and reformers of the church age.

Because of this intense persecution against Pentecostals, to add to this a battle with the powerful forces of segregation and bigotry, was understandably more than many felt they could handle at the time. Military history teaches that to try to fight a two-front war will almost always result in defeat, so the battle against racism in the church would have to wait for another generation while the early Pentecostals devoted themselves to making a way for the baptism in the Holy Spirit.

Even so, we must not forget that the Pentecostal Movement began with those from every race, every creed and social position, in unity, seeking the Lord together. The power that was released to impact the world has never been as great as it was in those first years at Azusa when this unity existed. It is apparent that the Pentecostal/Charismatic Movement, and indeed the church, will never come into its full potential until this unity is permanent.

From the first Day of Pentecost in the beginning of the Book of Acts, the Holy Spirit has proven that He will only come to the degree that we have unity. Like those who came to the Azusa Street Mission, we must want the Holy Spirit more than we want to hold on to our differences. Christianity was born as a multi-cultural entity, on the Day of Pentecost when men had gathered from **"every nation" (see Acts 2:5)**. It was fitting that this is the way that the Holy Spirit came again at Azusa.

In the little group at Antioch which sent out the first missionaries to the Gentiles, there were representatives from different races and social positions. When the Lord wants to do something truly great on the earth, this seems to be a requirement. In its most pure form the church will always be multi-cultural. That is why Paul had to resolutely confront Peter concerning his hypocrisy of not eating with the Gentiles. Racial equality before God is fundamental to the Gospel, and even Peter **"stood condemned" (see Galatians 2:11)** if he had fallen to this basic deception that tries to divide the church and humanity.

It is debatable whether this multi-racial nature of the church was lost by the church because of her drift into apostasy, or whether it caused that drift. Regardless, it was the true state of the church that was born on the Day of

Pentecost when the Holy Spirit first came to the church. It was the state of the church that gave birth to the modern Pentecostal Revival, and we will only be the true church to the degree that we recover it. This is being realized by many church leaders today, and overcoming racism is now rightly a major thrust almost across the spectrum of Christianity. This is certainly one of the most positive signs of our times.

The Lord is the "Blessed Creator" who so loves diversity that He made every snowflake, every leaf on every tree, as well as every one of us different. In all of this diversity one of the great marvels of the creation is the harmony and balance that is found throughout it. Every species of every plant and animal all have a part to play in keeping the whole going. The same is true of man. God made men in His image, and gave different aspects of His nature as gifts to different races and cultures. We all need each other to be the complete reflection of Him. That is why His house must be **"a house of prayer for all the nations" (see Mark 11:17)**. The word often translated **"nations"** in the New Testament, including this text, is the Greek *ethnos*, from which we derive our English word "ethnic." The Lord's house must include all ethnic groups. We will never be who we were created to be as the church until this is a reality.

CHAPTER NINETEEN
WHERE THE SPIRIT IS, THERE IS LIBERTY

There is another great aspect to Seymour's remarkable leadership at Azusa. This was his ability to discern and trust the Holy Spirit's leadership, and give Him the freedom that He requires. In spite of almost constant pressure from world-renowned church leaders, who came from around the globe to impose what they perceived to be needed for order and direction on the young revival, for nearly two years Seymour held the course and allowed the Holy Spirit to move in His own, often mysterious, ways. Like Evan Roberts, who was at the same time leading the great Welsh Revival, Seymour's greatest leadership quality was his ability to *follow* the Holy Spirit.

Seymour and Roberts both believed that the Holy Spirit required the freedom to move through whomever He chose, not just the leadership. They both resolved to allow anyone to be used by the Lord, even the most humble believers. This sometimes brought embarrassment as immature believers took advantage of this liberty, but more often it allowed the Holy Spirit to do marvelous things among them. If we really want the Holy Spirit in our midst, we must allow Him to be the leader. He is, after all, God.

THE CHOICE

Finding the balance between God's sovereignty and the free will of man has been one of the most ancient debates in the church. However, they are both true, and they are not in conflict with each other. They are both one hundred percent true. God is utterly sovereign, and He has also in His sovereignty delegated authority to men that He will not even violate Himself.

Without freedom, there could be no true worship or true obedience. That is why the Lord placed the Tree of the Knowledge of Good and Evil in the Garden. There could be no true obedience if there was not also the freedom to disobey. The Lord is the unquestioned Sovereign of the universe, but when He delegates authority, He does not even violate it Himself. Otherwise we would never be able to rule and reign with Him. To rule requires both authority and responsibility. Therefore, though He always knows what we need even before we ask Him, He always waits for us to ask.

For this reason, "**...where the Spirit of the Lord is, there is liberty**" **(II Corinthians 3:17).** Liberty is required for true worship or true obedience. He has removed the veil into His presence for all, but we must seek Him. Therefore, we are all as close to God as we want to be. We are also as far from Him as we choose to be. If His manifest presence is not in our midst, it is not because of Him but because of our own choice.

Many give lip service to wanting the Holy Spirit to lead their meetings, but they really are not willing to give up their own programs, or to trust Him in the way that He requires if He is to do this. Seymour was willing.

This kind of "hands off" leadership style has been a hallmark of most of the world's great revivals. However, even a cursory study of church history reveals that outside of revival it has seldom, if ever, worked. God simply moves in different ways at different times. In times of true revival there are usually dramatic and unique demonstrations of His sovereignty, and it is best to just stay out of His way. The rest of the time He seems to delight most in working with and through men. Even so, our goal should always be to submit our will to His and always follow His leading. The more we can do this, the more He will usually manifest His wonderful presence.

As Vance Havner once observed, "Revival is like a sale at the department store. It is more dramatic and gets more press, but the normal business of the store is the day-to-day merchandising of products." Revivals are likewise much more spectacular, but they are not the normal business of the church. Much more has been accomplished for the overall advancement of the Gospel by the day-to-day witnessing of faithful saints and by the service of faithful pastors in local churches, who day-by-day fight on the front lines of the battle against darkness, than has ever been accomplished by a revival.

Revivals have sparked great spiritual advances, but they are sustained only by the day-to-day devotion of the saints. This is likewise the story of the Pentecostal/Charismatic Movement. Azusa was spectacular, as were other subsequent revivals and movements, but the real and substantial advance has come from a multitude of lesser-known, but nevertheless, faithful leaders and people. Their advances may have been less dramatic, but over the long-term, their faithful plodding ahead has accomplished far more.

The same is true in our personal lives. Spectacular, spiritual experiences are wonderful and can propel us to great heights of devotion and worship. Even so, the real strength of every Christian's life will usually be found in the degree of faithfulness to the disciplines of Bible study, prayer, fellowship, and day-to-day witnessing.

In times of revival, there is also a dynamic, manifest presence of the Holy Spirit that makes deviations apparent to almost everyone, including those who make them. Needed corrections are therefore usually automatic. However, when we do not have this dynamic presence of the Lord that is found in revival, almost every vacuum of leadership will be quickly filled with the immature, the prideful, or the rebellious. The result of this will not be revival, but confusion, which is then usually joined by sin and heresy.

It is important that we do not "get the cart in front of the horse" in the leadership we use. Seymour could use the leadership style that he did *because* he had revival. If he had tried to use this style with the same number and types of people without the dynamic of revival present, he would have had chaos. This has happened to many who have tried to exhibit revival-type leadership without revival. The key is to be ready to step aside when the presence of the Lord does come.

Our goal should be to have such a manifest presence of the Lord in all of our meetings. However, the way to do this is not to just sit back and do nothing until He comes, but to faithfully press on to maturity by seeking to increasingly be sensitive to His leading. Occasionally, the Lord catches us up in a spectacular manifestation of His presence, but He usually leads us to higher ground like a father teaching his child to walk. He will help us to stand, and then He backs off so that we must walk to Him. As we learn to take a couple of steps, He backs farther away so that we have to walk farther. He is not just playing with us when He removes His manifest presence; He is teaching us to walk in the Spirit and to pursue Him. When we do not feel Him, it is not a time to sit down, but to try to take more steps.

The New Testament epistles are basically the apostles' exhortations to leaders who were serving in times that were not dynamic revivals. They did not expect the Spirit to come every day like He did on the Day of Pentecost, so they went about doing the day-to-day work of the ministry. However, when He does decide to come in a dramatic way that ignites a revival, it is time to drop what we are doing and ride the wave for as far as it will take us.

Wisdom is to know when the Lord is telling us to go forth and take the land, sword in hand and when He is telling us to stand and watch His salvation. There are times for each. Anytime we try to use the wrong strategy in the wrong place, we will have problems. God's strategy is not one or the other, but both, which demands that we seek Him for every situation.

Seymour was called to lead in a revival. For a time he exemplified the remarkable wisdom of just staying in prayer and letting the Lord do the leading (he actually kept his head in a box during the meetings so that his prayer would not be distracted by all that was going on). However, the fierce persecution that raised up against the movement soon pressured him into an increasingly protectionist stature. Gradually he allowed more and more control of the meetings to be taken over by a few leaders. Soon they were following a program for the meetings. Those who were witnesses said that just as gradually as this happened, the Holy Spirit seemed to depart.

This explanation of how the revival at Azusa Street ended seems to be accurate. However, it is also possible that it was simply time to move on, and that the Spirit was withdrawing His presence so that the people would go forth. Just as the sale at a department store would lose its impact if it went on all of the time, it does not seem that the Lord ever intended for revivals to last in their initial form forever.

It is true that most revivals do end prematurely, or in a way that is not preferable. This usually happens because of human mistakes. We should learn from these, but let us also not fall into the trap of wrongly worshiping revival. Even without revival we can be as close to the

Lord today as anyone ever has been. The issue is not whether to seek revival or not, but to seek the Lord and His will.

Without question, the Azusa Street Revival was one of the greatest in all of church history. It can be argued that it has not yet ended, but has gone on in many different forms and in many different places. It is right for us to give honor to whom honor is due, and William J. Seymour is rightly considered one of the greatest Christian leaders of all time. He was a great leader for as long as he maintained the leadership style to which *he* was called, not taking initiative, but being sensitive to the leading of the Holy Spirit.

For the Azusa Street part of this study, I borrowed heavily from Frank Bartleman's own account of the revival in his classic work, Another Wave of Revival, now published by Whitaker House Publishers. This book contains many important insights on the nature of revival and can be found in many Christian bookstores.

CHAPTER TWENTY

THE ATOMIC AGE OF THE SPIRIT

O ver the last two millenniums, the church has
experienced many revivals, renewals, and reformation movements. Like the Welsh Revival, some
have been used to spur the entire church to spiritual
advancement. In its far-reaching impact on the world
and the church, none have equaled the Azusa Street
Revival which began in 1906. One hundred years later
its influence is not only felt, but is continuing to
increase. The seed of almost every subsequent revival,
renewal, or reformation movement can be traced to it.
Just as the pattern for a mature oak tree can be found in
the genetic code of its acorn, the pattern of what the church
is becoming today can be seen at Azusa Street. This is
why understanding this revival is crucial for us today.

Even though such movements are inevitably called
"new" when they first appear, they have actually been a
progressive restoration of the biblical truth, which was

lost or neglected during the Middle Ages. At the turn of the century, remnants of the great restoration movements merged, forming a "critical mass." This resulted in gospel explosions that shook the world. The two greatest of these were in Wales and Los Angeles. Together they would ignite powerful changes in the way Christianity was manifested on the earth.

Through the Pentecostal Revival and the subsequent neo-Pentecostal movements spawned from it, such as the Charismatic, Third Wave, and other restoration movements, more ministers of the Gospel have been ordained, more missionaries have been sent out, more churches have been planted, and more people have been brought to salvation than through any other movement in church history. Studies estimate that nearly 90 percent of all new converts to Christianity are now coming to Christ through the Pentecostal/Charismatic Movements.

To call what began at Azusa Street in Los Angeles just a revival is to obscure its true importance. It was a revival, but it was also a renewal movement, and it resulted in an accelerated reformation of the church. As stated, overall, there may not have been another movement in history that has had a greater impact on the entire church. Its influence has now spanned every denomination and movement to the degree that it would be impossible to understand the present church, or its future, without understanding this movement.

THE SPEED OF LIGHT

The beginning of the twentieth century marked the rapid increase of knowledge that the Lord had predicted would come at the end of the age. It has been estimated that it took 5,900 years of man's recorded history for our knowledge of the universe to double. It then doubled again in just decades. It is now doubling every couple of years! As the Apostle Paul wrote in I Corinthians 15:46, **"However, the spiritual is not first, but the natural; then the spiritual."** Running parallel to this great increase of knowledge in the natural has been a similarly astonishing recovery of truth in Christianity. The difference is that the Information Age is being fueled by new discoveries, while the great spiritual renewal of the church is being fueled by the rediscovery of the truth that Jesus and His apostles taught.

The Bible itself is more infinite in its scope and depth than anything discovered in the natural world. In recent years, a hidden code was found in the Bible that has astonished the world's greatest scientific minds. The code has such depth and intricacies that it forced even the most vehement secular scientists to declare "We are not alone!" One stated that the Creator of the Bible code is not only far beyond any human mind, but far beyond even a mind that we can conceive of at this time. Though it took a computer to discover the code, it has been estimated that if every computer in the world were linked together, they still would not have the power to create even the rudiments of this code. The discovery of the Dead Sea Scrolls verified that the Bible code was implanted in the Scriptures at least two thousand years ago, but we know it was placed there by the Creator when He gave His people His Word. It is just one more witness of how awesome our God is.

It is interesting that many of these great minds studying the Bible code are now sure that we are not alone, and that there is an intellect in the universe which is beyond even our ability to comprehend at this time. Yet, they have not put it together that this great intellect is simply the God who wrote the Bible, which the code is found in! The cold, hard fact that God did this, is slapping them in the face every day, but they still cannot see Him. However, this, too, reveals an important biblical truth. Even those with the greatest human intellect cannot find God unless the Holy Spirit leads them. We need the Holy Spirit to know the truth, and to worship God the way that He wants to be worshiped.

Running parallel to the great darkness that keeps even the greatest human geniuses from seeing God, the Holy Spirit is being poured out in an unprecedented way, leading unprecedented multitudes to a saving knowledge of Jesus. At the present, people are being born-again at a rate higher than the natural birthrate in some parts of the world. There is an explosion of both natural and spiritual knowledge, but presently they are on two different tracks, leading sometimes in opposite directions.

The Bible code was planted in the Bible by God for a reason, but Christians do not need it. The plain text of the Bible has limitless depth and intricacies that are far beyond what any human mind could have devised, or to comprehend without the Holy Spirit. The plain text of the Bible is a far higher knowledge than the code. It does not just reveal what God has done, or is doing, but why.

By studying the plain text of the Bible, we can get to know the very Person of God. Through His relationships to men and women that are recorded in the Bible, we can clearly know and understand what He expects of us. With this knowledge we can serve Him, worship Him, and live lives that are pleasing to Him. Our goal must be to know Him, but not just know Him, we must also do His will.

The Bible is a treasure of unfathomable value. Every "discovery" mined from its pages results in great, sweeping changes in the world. Democracy, free enterprise, and even science itself have their roots in the discovery, or rediscovery, of truths. The overwhelming majority of the positive influences in civilization can be traced to the Bible. Just as the increase of knowledge in the natural has brought such sweeping changes in the natural, there is an increase of spiritual knowledge being released which is bringing great sweeping changes in the church, as well as society in general.

The changes coming from the increase of spiritual knowledge are not changes in the basic truths upon which Christianity is built, and which will always stand as unchanging. Neither are they in any way bringing changes in biblical morality and integrity. These, too, are ageless and will never change.

Neither are the changes an attempt to conform Christianity to modern times. Some of them are in fact an expanding and deepening of our biblical and historical moorings. Some of the changes are resulting in the expansion of strategies for fulfilling the Great Commission, but that is still not the main thrust of the change. The greatest source of this spiritual increase of knowledge is simply a deeper revelation of the person of Jesus Christ, and the changes are simply an increasing conformity to His image.

In a very real way, Jesus is Jacob's ladder, which Jesus Himself confirmed when He said to Nathaniel:

> **"Because I said to you that I saw you under the fig tree, do you believe? You shall see greater things than these."**

> **And He said to him, "Truly, truly, I say to you, you shall see the heavens opened, and the angels of God ascending and descending on the Son of Man" (John 1:50-51).**

This was a direct reference to the ladder that Jacob had seen, as recorded in Genesis 28:12-13:

> **And he** (Jacob) **had a dream, and behold, a ladder was set on the earth with its top reaching to heaven; and behold, the angels of God were ascending and descending on it.**

> **And behold, the LORD stood above it and said, "I am the LORD, the God of your father Abraham and the God of Isaac; the land on which you lie, I will give it to you and to your descendants.**

Jesus is Jacob's ladder in the sense that the messengers of God ascend into the heavenly places by a progressive revelation of Him. As we behold more of

His glory, we are changed more into His image. The result of true spiritual knowledge is not some esoteric understanding, but it is being changed into the nature of Christ. Knowing Him better is how we ascend into the heavenly places to sit with Him, and how we descend to the earth to represent Him.

The great revivals now taking place around the world are all the result of an increasing devotion to a personal relationship with Jesus Christ, which is the result of the increasing receptivity to the Holy Spirit, who was given to lead us to Jesus. This great, world-wide receptivity to the Holy Spirit by the church largely began in Wales, but was truly sown abroad with the Azusa Street Revival of 1906.

The Scriptures are clear that the Lord is going to return for a bride who is without spot or wrinkle (see Ephesians 5:27). She will be pure, holy, unified, and so powerful that the nations will tremble at her presence. Many look at the outward conditions of the church and think that this is impossible, or if it can be done, it will take a thousand years. However, as Peter asserted in II Peter 3:8: **"But do not let this one fact escape your notice, beloved, that with the Lord one day is as a thousand years, and a thousand years as one day."** The Lord can do in one day what we think would take a thousand years. God can speed things up, and He is.

In the natural and spiritual realms, change is accelerating. Those who resist change in either realm are breaking and being discarded like old wineskins.

Movements, denominations, and churches that stop moving are now dying very fast. Those who learn to ride the wave of the Holy Spirit grow at a rate unthinkable just years ago. In the midst of this great increasing pace of change, there are traditions and historic moorings that can help us navigate through these changes more safely, but we must not let them become anchors that stop our progress. The cloud of God's presence is moving forward at a very fast pace.

For mostly economic purposes, the world has devised a very efficient way to process and make useful its new discoveries. In general, the church has not done as well, and many of the great truths that should have been the domain of the church have been stolen by the world and put to less-than-noble-use. For example, almost every musical style has been born in the church; and then the world has quickly stolen it, merchandised it, and used it to promote its own evil philosophy instead of it being used by the church to spread the Gospel, as God intended. Even science and modern education were born in the church, and were given for the accomplishing of the Great Commission, but they have been hijacked!

It is time that the church learns to recognize the time of its visitations and not let them be stolen by the world any longer. It is also time to take back what was stolen, and as is the standard of the Law, make the thief pay back seven times that which was stolen. Science will be reclaimed by the church and become seven times more effective and accurate than what the world has been able to do with it because all true science will lead to the Creator. Education will be taken back by the church and become seven times more effective than it ever was when the world was its jailer. The church will set it free to be what it was created to be, but first the church *must* be set free to be what she was created to be.

We are not going through changes just for the sake of change; rather the church is headed for a certain destiny. We must define both where we are going and why. We must also, as the Parable of the Talents exhorts us, learn to manage the great treasures of knowledge that are entrusted to us, so that the maximum benefit is made of them.

Even so, all that is going on spiritually today is far beyond any human ability to manage. The Lord Jesus is the Head of His church, and He is the only One who can manage His own household. However, He does delegate. There is a desperate need for all who are called to leadership to have deep roots and clear vision if we are going to stay close to Him through this incredible time of change that we are now in, and properly manage what has been delegated to us. This requires understanding.

It is not enough for us to just "take more spiritual land." We must be able to hold what we take. As Proverbs 24:3-4 states:

> **By wisdom a house is built, and by understanding it is established;**

> **And by knowledge the rooms are filled with all precious and pleasant riches.**

This great increase of knowledge can fill our houses, but it is going to first take wisdom to build the houses. Then we need understanding to establish them. Our goal must be more than just having large churches; it must be to have a house that God wants to dwell in. Our goal must be to see a church without spot or wrinkle, a glorious bride prepared for the coming of the King. What good is the most glorious temple if the Lord is not in it?

Just a couple of centuries ago, great battles were fought over the rights of individual Christians to be free to read their own Bibles. Thousands upon thousands, if not millions, died in these wars, even though only a fraction of them were literate and could read a Bible if they had the right. They did this for our sakes. Regardless of what we attain to in our time, we are standing on the shoulders of all who went before us, who fought and took the land of which we are now eating the fruit. Even though they may have also made some glaring mistakes, they are worthy of honor.

Today most Christians have several Bibles. Now we are bombarded with spiritual knowledge and revelations of truth to the degree that not even the largest mega-church could absorb them all, much less apply them. But that is alright. No one church is supposed to. We each have a part to play, and we need to stay focused on our part. Even so, it does help for us to have at least a concept of the "big picture," or where the whole church is headed.

We must also "honor our fathers and mothers" so that our days may be long upon the earth (see Deuteronomy

5:16). Many great revivals and spiritual movements die prematurely because they neglect to honor those that have gone before us, which is so crucial to the Lord. This was the only commandment that He gave with a promise attached, which was longevity. To do this, we must acknowledge that our progress is largely due to the faith and courage of our spiritual fathers and mothers. Heritage is important, which is why the Lord instructed every generation of Israel to celebrate certain feasts in remembrance of what God had done in previous generations.

Even though we must be committed to honoring our spiritual parents, the Lord was not just called "the God of Abraham," but "the God of Abraham, Isaac, and Jacob," which means that He wants to relate to every generation. We want to honor our spiritual parents, but we must also have our own encounters with Him.

Therefore, we are studying the Welsh and Azusa Street Revivals for understanding, for honoring our spiritual forefathers, but also to have our hearts stirred in such a way that we, too, must have our own encounters with the Lord. We are not content to just recount the stories, but we must see God move again. Just as Frank Bartleman said that he would rather die than not see revival, we must have a like passion to see God move in our own lives.

God is moving. We are well into "the atomic age of the Spirit." As stated, the pace of spiritual change has already exceeded the ability of men to even understand all that is going on, much less try to implement it all.

However, the release of different movements and the interchange between them, the timing of the release of rediscovered truth, combined with the conditions in the world, make it clear that the Spirit is very much in control. It is simply no longer possible for anyone to understand it all, in the natural or spiritual realms. Even so, to understand the essence of these movements is essential for anyone who is called to leadership in these times, if we are going to be responsive to what the Spirit is doing in these times.

Of course, there are many individuals, churches, and even whole denominations that were birthed out of this movement that have stopped moving. In many places one can only find the remnants of the past glory, with little or no continuing fire. However, around the world there are multitudes of Pentecostal/Charismatic churches that are ablaze with the presence and activity of God. In countries where the greatest advances of the Gospel are now taking place, Pentecostal and/or Charismatic churches are inevitably found at the vanguard.

Like most others, the Pentecostal Movement had a spectacular beginning, followed by upheaval from within and persecution from without. Many mistakes were made that threatened to sidetrack the entire movement. These were almost always resolved in such a way that they gave even greater stability to the movement, enabling it to continue its advance. The lessons we learn from these situations can help any advancing church or movement.

Understanding the mistakes made by others can help us to avoid the same traps. However, before we become too concerned with how to avoid the traps of revival, we need to know how to start one! Because the most important step in any journey is the first one, understanding how true moves of God begin is crucial. That is the essence of this study. We have looked at some mistakes, but we should be far more concerned with what was done right. To take but a few hours to study our history can save us years of being sidetracked in the future.

In all that we study, we must recognize that the Seed of the church is Jesus Christ. We can look at Him now and know what we are to look like. When we study the Scriptures, the church, or history, He is the One that we must be looking for. It was reportedly said that after Michelangelo had finished his great sculpture of King David, he was asked how he did it. He replied that he had a picture of King David in his heart and cut away all of the stone that wasn't him. In a sense, that is what those who are called to be "master builders" in the church must do. We must have a clear picture of Jesus in our hearts and remove everything that is not Him. This is likewise what we will seek to do with this important history.

CHAPTER TWENTY-ONE

SUMMARY

Because our goal is not to just honor the past, but to prepare for our own times, there are some basic principles about revivals that are especially illuminated in these two revivals. In a sense, this might be considered plowing the soil before planting the seeds, but it is necessary if we are to get the full benefit of these most remarkable histories.

Revival is not really what we are seeking as much as the Lord, but those who find Him will inevitably ignite revivals. Revivals are the fruit of lives that are lived for Him, loving Him, seeking Him, and abiding in Him. Becoming consumed with how to manage the revival, rather than continuing our pursuit of Him, is one of the ways that many revivals fade away, and in some cases grind to a halt. One of the most tragic failures and errors of those who begin to experience revival is the foolish pursuit of trying to keep people excited. As Peter Lord likes to say, "The main thing is to keep the main thing the main thing," and the main thing is the pursuit of God. Don't ever lose that—it is our greatest treasure.

The greatest move of God, since God Himself walked the earth through the Person of His Son, is yet to come. The Lord Himself called this the harvest that will be the end of the age. This greatest harvest of all will be the result of the preaching of the Gospel of the kingdom throughout the earth (see Matthew 13:39). Together the Welsh Revival and the Azusa Street Revival give us a very good foretaste of what this will be like.

It is usually very hard to look at a seed and understand the great plant or tree that it can become. You can count the seeds in an apple, but who can count the apples in a seed? Therefore, I will try not to over-define what we are to expect, but there is one thing we do know. As great as the Welsh and Azusa Street Revivals were, they were not the end of the age, and so the harvest has not yet come. Therefore, they were not the mature fruit. As much as we may marvel at these, there is more yet to come!

HE IS STILL BORN IN STABLES

In biblical times, the stable was a most offensive place. The floors were composed of decades worth of compacted dung and other filth. The stench was so great that they were placed as far away from other dwellings as possible. By today's standards, they would not even be fit for animals. That the Lord of Glory would choose such a place to make His entry into this world is one of the more profound revelations of His message to man. We would do well not to miss His point, as He has not stopped using such places to make His appearances. Just as the Lord chose Wales, the least of the principalities of the British Isles, He later chose the tiny little Azusa Street Mission and three humble, but courageous, black pastors to change the face of modern Christianity.

Human reasoning would never lead us to a stable to find God. The only way He could be found was by revelation; only those who were led by the Spirit would come. This has not changed. That which has been born of God is usually repulsive to the pride and presumptions of men. The Lord has never birthed a true revival out of the great theological centers and bastions of influence. **"God resists the proud, but gives grace to the humble" (see James 4:6 NKJV).** The more humble we are, the more grace we can receive.

After His birth, Jesus was then raised in the most despised town in the most despised nation of Israel. Even His physical appearance was such that no one would be attracted to Him (see Isaiah 53:2). He then left this world after the most degrading torture and execution yet devised by the base and demented schemes of fallen men. This Gospel is foolishness to the natural man, and it always will be. It will never attract those who live by human wisdom or those who are attracted by the pride of political influence. Only those who love truth more than anything else in this world will walk with Him in the reproach of the true gospel.

The birth, life, and death of Jesus put the ax to the root of the tree of human wisdom and pride—the fruit of the Tree of the Knowledge of Good and Evil. It is the most powerful message the creation has ever heard; it is the most profound testimony of the character and nature of God. When we embellish this Gospel to make it appeal to carnal men, we destroy its power to set them free, and we ourselves begin to drift from the path of life. For this reason, Paul preached nothing but Christ and Him crucified. He knew that if men were to come by any other message their conversions would be false.

To see what the Lord is doing, we may have to go to places that require the death of our flesh and sometimes our reputations. We must have the heart of Simeon and Anna, who could see in a mere infant the salvation of the world. Do not be discouraged if the fruit is not yet apparent; look for the seed that will become the fruit. This does not mean that He is found only in the poor, the wretched, and the despised, but that is where He is usually found. **"But God has chosen the foolish things of the world to shame the wise, and God has chosen the weak things of the world to shame the things which are strong" (I Corinthians 1:27).**

The true Gospel will never appeal to the carnal nature of man—it will confront that nature and put the ax to its root. As the apostle declared, **"If I were still trying to please men, I would not be a bond-servant of Christ" (see Galatians 1:10).** We must choose who we are going to please. It will be Christ or man, but it will never be both. If we are not willing to embrace that which appears foolish to the worldly wise, we will not embrace that which God is doing. Again the church is facing a radical choice—will we preach a gospel that appeals to men while leaving their souls in jeopardy? Or will we preach the gospel that will change the hearts and save the souls of those who will humble themselves to receive it? In Wales and at Azusa Street they chose God, and the whole world has benefited from their choice.

CHILDREN OPENED THE GATES

In the small principality of Wales, a band of children and youth touched heaven and brought it to earth with such power that it quickly became front-page news around the world. The world's greatest authors, missionaries, theologians, and spiritual statesmen boarded ships and sailed from the four corners of the earth to sit at the feet of mostly teenagers, who were leading this remarkable move of God. Evan Roberts, the leader of the revival, was only twenty-seven, and most of his workers were far younger, but these were the "elders" who opened the gates for this revival, and then sat in those gates as judges. As the Lord said in Matthew 18:3-6:

> **"Truly I say to you, unless you are converted and become like children, you shall not enter the kingdom of heaven.**
>
> **"Whoever then humbles himself as this child, he is the greatest in the kingdom of heaven.**
>
> **"And whoever receives one such child in My name receives Me;**

but whoever causes one of these little ones who believe in Me to stumble, it is better for him that a heavy millstone be hung around his neck, and that he be drowned in the depth of the sea."

The great men of God of the time, such as G. Campbell Morgan, the pastor of the famous Westminster Chapel, and General Booth, founder of the Salvation Army, both came and humble themselves to sit at the feet of the children who were leading this revival. These were great in the kingdom. Others came with the spiritual pride of thinking that these children needed their guidance, and, one of these actually even became a stumbling block for the whole revival.

The point is that when revival breaks out, never go to it thinking it needs you, but just go opening your heart to how you can learn. Just as Uzzah died for his presumption of trying to steady the ark of God when the oxen stumbled as David was trying to bring it to Jerusalem (see II Samuel 6:6), it is a terrible presumption for us to think that we can steady the glory of God. God may in fact use us to help, but we are foolish to touch the glory without clear guidance from Him, regardless of how shaky things may seem to be.

THE LIGHT OF THE WORLD

For a brief period of time, heaven so pervaded Wales that the whole of Welsh society was more profoundly changed than has ever happened on the earth before. Even the first century church did not have the impact on local society that the Welsh Revival did for a time. During the Welsh Revival, not only did the demons flee and sin become unthinkable, every other devotion in life but the pursuit of God simply lost its appeal to even those who before had seemed the most hardened sinners.

Possibly the greatest result of the Welsh Revival was that a deep, yearning, passionate hunger for God was spread throughout the earth. During the period of this revival God and His works seemed to be the main conversation almost anywhere on the planet that you went. In many places, churches were open for seven nights a week and still they could not contain the people. Bibles and Christian books were not only the bestsellers of the times—they were just about the only sellers. Hunger for the knowledge of God suddenly gripped the earth.

As we have covered, during this time possibly the most spiritually hungry of all was the young black man named William Seymour. As it was said of him that he wanted God more than he wanted oxygen, he may have been one of the most desperate seekers of God to have walked the earth since Enoch. Such people will always find God, and they are almost always used to spread the wonder of Him throughout the earth, Seymour was certainly used that way.

No two revivals are exactly alike, but there is almost always a divine link, a connection, among them all. To be a part of the next there does seem to almost always be a rediscovery of the ones who went before. It was no accident that Evan Roberts, the leader of the Welsh Revival, communicated by letter directly to Bartleman and Seymour. The leaders of the new revival had to be baptized by the leader of the former one, and they were not only by Robert's letters, but by all the books and tracts they read and spread around about the Welsh Revival.

Just hearing the stories about the revivals, or reading about them, inevitably stirs others to seek the Lord in a new and fresh way. The fire on these moves of God was so intense that when letters or newspaper articles about them were read in other parts of the world, revival would break out there. The stories of these events are simply so electric that even the hardest heart cannot help but to be jolted by them. Today, a century after they happened, there is still such a fire on just the reports of these revivals. Those who read or hear them cannot help but to be still impacted with conviction and hope, and true hope will never disappoint.

THE SOURCE OF GRACE

Because revivals often seem to spread uncontrollably, there is going to be a temptation on the part of many to try to control them. This can be a foolish and devastating mistake. This does not mean that we should not use the authority that God gives us when we are used to ignite or be a part of the leadership of revival, but as we are warned in Proverbs 11:2-3 and 16:18:

**When pride comes, then comes dishonor,
but with the humble is wisdom.**

The integrity of the upright will guide them....

Pride goes before destruction, and a haughty spirit before stumbling.

As we are also exhorted in I Corinthians 1:26-31:

For consider your calling, brethren, that there were not many wise according to the flesh, not many mighty, not many noble;

but God has chosen the foolish things of the world to shame the wise, and God has chosen the weak things of the world to shame the things which are strong,

and the base things of the world and the despised, God has chosen, the things that are not, that He might nullify the things that are,

that no man should boast before God.

But by His doing you are in Christ Jesus, who became to us wisdom from God, and righteousness and sanctification, and redemption,

that, just as it is written, "Let him who boasts, boast in the Lord."

We do want to examine the many subtle but important principles that seem to always be found near the heart of true revival. However, this pursuit is so that we can ourselves prepare for the greater revival that is coming—the harvest that is the end of this age. One of the ways we can best prepare is by resolving to walk in the humility which our calling demands of true wisdom.

We were more likely called because of being foolish than for our great wisdom. Therefore, we should lean even more on the Lord, seeking His wisdom, and not walking in the presumption of thinking we are the "man of power for the hour."

The greatest part of Bible prophecy focuses on this period and the significant events in church history are all to some degree in preparation for it. We are here living in these times for this purpose, and the Lord has gifted us accordingly, but all of the gifts of God operate by His grace, and as I will repeat once again, as we are told in James 4:6, **"God is opposed to the proud, but gives grace to the humble."** Therefore, we must always keep this knowledge that regardless of how much we have been gifted, grace is what we need, and we will only keep His grace as long as we keep a humble heart.

Yet, the church is not here to be an observer, but the light of the world. We are not called to be a thermometer, but a thermostat. We are not here just to interpret world events, but to set their course. Of course, this would be the most arrogant attitude Christians could have if it were not appointed by God. He has also set the way in which this must be done to keep the true on the path. It must be accomplished by the power of the truth and the conviction of lives that reflect that truth.

The Lord has also guaranteed persecution as a fire to keep His followers true, consuming the wood, hay, and stubble in the church, and purifying the gold, silver, and precious stones. Though the Welsh Revival enjoyed some of the most positive press that possibly any move of God ever has, they were also continually attacked and ridiculed in the media. The Azusa Street Revival was more typical of revivals as very few positive articles appeared about it in the media, and it was viciously and continually attacked. However, even the media attacks served to spread the word and helped to draw so many to the revival that, for a time, it was said that Azusa Street was the most famous address in the world.

THE LIGHT IN THEIR TIME

There are prophetic parallels found in the Welsh and Azusa Street Revivals that can help to guide us in the necessary preparation for these times. The church in Wales and Los Angeles, and the communities of Wales and Los Angeles in that time, are parallels of the church today, and the condition of society today—especially in the sense that both were experiencing a great secularization and meltdown of morality. These revivals helped to turn this tide back for several decades.

Just as a map is useless unless you know where you are on the map, we need to understand history to know where we are in God's plan. The Bible is basically two-thirds history, and one-third prophecy, much of which has now been fulfilled, so that prophecy is now history too. It is the most accurate map that can show us where we have been, where we are now, and where we are going. These two revivals are major signposts on that map.

Understanding how the spiritual foundation was laid for this great revival can help us to understand the foundation that the Lord is today laying in His church to prepare for the coming harvest. Understanding what was done correctly can help us to do the right things. Likewise, honestly looking at the mistakes can help us to avoid making the same ones—as a wise man once stated: "Those who do not know history are doomed to repeat it."

PREPARE THE WAY

In just the last two decades, the world has experienced the greatest harvest of souls in its history. Most of it has come in Africa, South and Central America, and Asia, but the result has been, in some estimates, more people coming to salvation since 1988 than did from the Day of Pentecost until 1988. Some of this has to do with the fact that there are more people on the earth now than there have been in the rest of human history combined, but the world has also experienced the greatest harvest of souls in the last few years than ever before. However, as I warned in my book, *The Harvest*, this first wave was but the bringing in of the laborers for a coming worldwide revival that would be much greater.

There is a coming worldwide move of God that will be much greater, bringing between one and two billion new believers into the faith. This move of God will be different than any other in many ways. But in some ways it is the fruit of the Welsh and Azusa Street Revivals and will be like them, which is why we must study them. However, we cannot expect any revival to be exactly like these again. God, who likes to make even every snowflake different, loves diversity. As we can see in the New Testament, Jesus did not even seem to heal two people the same way.

FOCUS ON THE LIGHT, NOT THE DARKNESS

I have met and talked with quite a few people who have studied revivals to find out what went wrong with them so that we can avoid the same mistakes. That can be helpful, but I have never met anyone with this as a primary devotion who had any kind of revival breaking out around them. I agree that understanding the problems and mistakes of previous revivals can help us, but before we get so concerned about the mistakes, we need to find out what they did right that would enable the revival to break out in the first place!

There are many aspects of these great revivals that we should seek to emulate, and there are some we should avoid. It seems that the great interest which is now being stirred in the church to study history is part of the grace of God to help prepare us for it. Let us not neglect so great a grace.

As stated, we also need to understand the bridges between these two revivals. I have come to the conclusion that the Lord intended to do everything that was accomplished through the Welsh Revival in Wales. But a turn from the course was made in Wales, and another vessel and place had to be chosen for beginning of the modern Pentecostal Movement. When the Welsh leaders made the turn the revival quickly died, but immediately the fire erupted in Los Angeles. When that mission missed a turn and got off track, revival broke out in other places, and this pattern continues around the world to this day.

So our purpose is first to understand the seedbed of true revival so that we might have one, and then to seek, with humility, the grace of God to keep it going. However, even if we do start a revival that is destined to get off track at some point and end, it is better to have started it and accomplished what was accomplished than to have not had one at all.

For all that the Pentecostal Movement has helped to restore to the church, there is obviously more that the Lord is going to give to His people. Many Christian leaders, even some from Azusa Street, have maintained that there was more coming. What more could we expect than the baptism in the Holy Spirit?

Many of these leaders described what they were prophetically seeing as Azusa Street releasing the baptism in the Holy Spirit. But they were also seeing another move coming which would release the Holy Spirit *and* fire. At first I thought this was a matter of "splitting hairs" or "wrangling about words," which the Scriptures warn us not to do. However, as I kept coming across this same term "and" as well as the expectation for this move in the writings or messages of some of the greatest Christian leaders of the last century, and even those who were at Azusa Street, it began to have more merit. Now it seems that some of the new, emerging generation of leaders of today have been using the same term—that what is coming is the baptism of the Holy Spirit *and* fire. But what does this mean?

As we are told in I Corinthians 13, we see in part, know in part, and prophesy in part, so to have the whole picture we need to put our part together with what others have been given. This is the genius and glory of the church that one day will compel us together into a unity so great that the Lord will be able to trust us with unprecedented power and authority. In this study, I am trying to put the parts together from both Wales and Azusa, along with some others. To answer the question, as to what it means to be baptized in the Holy Spirit and fire, is a main purpose of this study, but it cannot be answered in a single statement now without tragically reducing its true meaning. There is a new Pentecost coming, again! This really is not new, but the recovery of some aspects of the baptism that are yet to be fully recovered by the modern Pentecostal and Charismatic Movements.

Of course, such a statement as this is bound to stir up controversy. However, such a belief has been at the foundation of possibly every move of God since the original Pentecostal outpouring of the Holy Spirit in the first century. To think that we have all there is to have, and that the church is all that it is called to be, is either an ultimate form of delusion, pride, or both.

I do not try to stir up controversy, but I seem to have a gift for doing this. I am fine with this because controversy seems necessary for true revival and has been at the core of every move of God in history, even when God Himself walked the earth. My goal is not to just talk about the past, but to see God do it again in our own time. The true message will always be challenged by the pretender (religious spirit) because it is the greatest threat to the dominance of that spirit in the church.

Even so, I am not implying that the baptism in the Holy Spirit, which has changed so many millions since Azusa Street is not real, but we do need to question if it is *all* that we are to expect. I have no doubt that the power is real, multitudes are being impacted, and great miracles are being experienced through the work of the Holy Spirit in our time. However, some major factors are missing—holiness, integrity, morality, and the holy fear of the Lord, which is the beginning and foundation of all true wisdom. These are the things that the great

Pentecostal leaders have often mentioned which came as a result of the baptism of fire. This fire was to both purify and give boldness.

In the Book of Acts, we see that the disciples were filled again on several occasions after the Day of Pentecost. Possibly the greatest of the additional fillings by the Spirit was boldness to be witnesses. It does seem that today many of the Pentecostal and Charismatic churches have lost the courage to speak the Word of God with boldness, without fear of the consequences, or who it offends, which was a hallmark of the baptism that came on the Day of Pentecost in the first century. If that is what happened to the first century apostles when they were baptized, where are their counterparts today?

Granted, many of the great modern Pentecostal fathers and mothers did have these characteristics in their life. But far too many fell into the ditches that are on either side of the path of life—either lawlessness or legalism. This trend continues to this day. However, there is a new stirring in the Spirit. There is something that is more basic and more profound, and it could be better compared to a new critical mass forming that will bring a release like unto a nuclear reaction.

A new Pentecost is coming. Again, this is not to, in any way, dishonor or fail to appreciate all that the great Welsh and Azusa Street Revivals opened the church up. In fact, just as Jesus had to be baptized by John to fulfill all righteousness before His own commissioning, it is crucial for all who will become a part of a new move, to submit to those who have gone before them, and honor them. At the same time, it is right for us to ask for more.

Since you have read the accounts of Wales and Azusa, I think you will concur that even though we have been blessed with many great moves of God since then, we just have not seen anything like these since. We can. You can.

Just as true faith in the Bible is not only believing that what is written in it is true, but it is believing to have the same things happen in our own lives—to truly honor these great revivals is to seek God with their zeal, focus, and resolve until they not only happen again, but in an even greater way.

Wales and Azusa were seeds. It is now time for the harvest. Our goal is more than just being inspired—it is to see them happen again in our own time. You may be the one God uses to strike the match that releases that fire. Why not? The Holy Spirit who is in you is not smaller or less powerful than the One who dwelt in the Apostle Paul, or anyone else. Why not you? Do not lose sight of the One who is behind these remarkable events, and the One whose favor will accomplish more than the greatest human efforts ever could. And He is in you!

The more humble and weak you are, the better candidate you may be for revival. When the Holy Spirit truly comes into the temple, all flesh and presumption flees! This was to be a hallmark of the Welsh Revival, for its time, and Azusa Street for its time. Great knowledge and eloquence bowed the knee to love and pure devotion, just as the "unlearned and untrained" apostles had stood before the Sanhedrin in Jerusalem and caused them all to marvel. One of the great preachers of that time was G. Campbell Morgan, the pastor of the illustrious Westminster Chapel, which is even today still considered one of the greatest pulpits in the world. Morgan testified that he would trade all of his learning for even a portion of the presence of God that accompanied these children. This was the common response as great pulpiteering, or the great leadership ability to mobilize people for the great spiritual projects of the time, seemed pale and looked insignificant in the presence of the anointing.

There is a great difference between preaching from a source of knowledge and preaching from a well of living water that flows from the throne of God. This was to be one of the central lessons of these two revivals. When God decides that He is going to move, He does not look for those who are wise enough or have enough education— He looks for those who are yielded and humble enough to risk following Him.

While the revival spread into almost every town and village of Wales, the ministry of Evan Roberts was mostly confined to just one of its twelve counties. The fire of God burned in many towns and villages which he did not visit. In many of the places which he did visit, he found the fire was already there. He would fan the flame a little and then go back to his base. Even Roberts knew from the beginning that he was not the source of what was happening. He simply tried to stay yielded to the Spirit so that he could play whatever part was required of him.

That the Lord has chosen men to be His habitation must be one of the great marvels of the whole creation. But God has also chosen men to *do* His work, and He often uses just a single individual to ignite a new move of His Holy Spirit. We see this in Scripture with such men as Peter, Paul, and John the Baptist. There are many historical examples of this principle such as Huss, Luther, Knox, Zinzendorf, Wesley, Edwards, Finney, and Seymour, who were used to ignite great spiritual advances. However, even though the Lord does often use a single individual to ignite the fires of revival or to lead a spiritual advance, there have always been others prepared to keep the fires going and to lay a proper foundation for the gains that are made.

Few men in history have been able to find that delicate balance between being used by God and trying to use God. A Christian teacher once defined *profanity* as "the seeking of one's own recognition at the expense of God's glory." Evan Roberts was driven by that conviction. He was utterly jealous to see that only the Lord received the glory. Seymour, though great in humility, was even more interested in keeping the hands of men off of the revival just because of his hunger to see God move. Both of these are needed by those who would be used in revival. For as long as they maintained this devotion, and as long as they required it of the other workers, the fires of revival continued to burn. From the beginning and until the end, neither of these revivals could be attributed to human charisma or promotional ability. When human charisma and promotions took over, the revivals quickly ended.

YOU DO NOT HAVE TO ADVERTISE A FIRE

A true move of God is not fueled by money, organization, or advertising. True revival only comes when the Pillar of Fire, that is the presence of God Himself, picks up and moves. To try to organize, promote, or sell a move of God is profane. Historians would later write that the most astonishing feature of the Welsh Revival was the lack of commercialism. There were no hymnbooks, no song leaders, no committees, no choirs, no great preachers, no offerings, and no organization. Yet souls were redeemed, families were healed, and whole cities were converted on a scale that had not been seen before or since.

James Stewart, a historian of the Welsh Revival, researched the newspapers and magazines published in Wales in 1904 and 1905, and he could not find a single advertisement promoting meetings. The only organized or planned evangelistic campaign for Evan Roberts was a single meeting in Liverpool in 1905. But even in that meeting the Lord disrupted the plans and radically changed the agenda before the evangelist arrived.

Broken plans seemed to be the hallmark of the Welsh Revival. Just weeks before it broke out in his home church in Loughor, Evan had planned campaigns throughout Wales with his brother Dan and a friend named Sydney Evans. Quickly, he discovered that the Spirit had another plan, and His plans were much better. Evan soon developed a healthy fear of man's planning and organization in the midst of revival.

This is not to imply that leadership and organization are not at times needed in the church, but when the Spirit is doing something new and fresh, the greatest gift is not knowing how to lead, but how to follow. The attempts at organization during the Welsh Revival all proved futile, and at times a hindrance to the true work.

It does seem that every time the Spirit wants to move in a creative way, He still has to find those who are "formless and void." Those with the humility that comes from knowing they do not have the answers, which stimulates a holy desperation for God in them, seem to be the only ones who can ever be responsive to the Lord when He wants to do a new thing. As the Lord Jesus explained to Nicodemus: **"The wind blows where it wishes and you hear the sound of it, but do not know where it comes from and where it is going; so is everyone who is born of the Spirit" (John 3:8).** The workers in the Welsh Revival came to understand that the Lord meant this literally.

Finally, they did not try to figure out where the Spirit was going next, they only tried to stay close enough to **"hear the sound of it" (see John 3:8).** The workers came to abhor the presumption that the Spirit would automatically go with them and bless their own plans. They knew that the Spirit did not follow them, but that they must follow the Spirit.

THE ILLUSION OF FOLLOWING THE SPIRIT

It is noteworthy that many who have tried to duplicate this kind of ministry style succumbed to spiritual delusions or even suffered the shipwreck of their faith. Even the apostles to the early church often planned their missionary journeys and would announce months ahead of time their impending visits. Yet, they always remained open for the Lord to change their plans. Nevertheless, the apostles could not always keep their intentions to visit a city, as with Paul's attempts to revisit the Corinthians.

The point is that our renewed minds are not in conflict with the Holy Spirit. The Lord did not lead the apostles around by the hand; He *sent* them. They made many of their own decisions because they had His mind. But because they were always growing and maturing, they did not always make the right decisions. At times the Lord would correct their course with an intervention of divine guidance through a dream, vision, or a prophet. We must labor with the spiritual wisdom that has been given to us, but always be open for the Lord to intervene and change our plans.

During times of a dynamic outpouring of the Holy Spirit, such as the Welsh Revival and at Azusa, the Lord can only use those who will yield themselves completely to Him, in order that He might do something entirely new. It seems that in every city the apostle Paul visited, the Holy Spirit moved differently than in the previous ones. Paul moved with vision, strategy, and decisiveness, but with a finely tuned sensitivity to the Holy Spirit and the willingness to yield to a different plan.

Many of the great missionary ventures in church history, such as William Booth's Salvation Army, were planned over many years, and they generally followed the plan. Those who might have worked with some of these missionary ventures would probably scorn the lack of organization of the Welsh and Azusa Revivals. Likewise, those who were a part of these revivals would almost certainly reject the seeming over-dependence on organization that such missionary societies had. However, both are valid ways that the Lord uses to guide His people.

A great tribute to General Booth was that he visited the Welsh Revival, observed that it was functioning in almost the opposite manner in which he ran the Salvation Army, and was still able to recognize that it was God and should not be tampered with. He then went back and continued to run the army just the way he had been, recognizing that God employs *different* strategies for different places or purposes.

Again, we must realize that God seldom moves the same way twice. It is His nature to be creative and diverse. We can learn much from the way the Lord moved in Wales and Azusa, and there are lessons for us all in the way that He moved through the Salvation Army in its early years. The Welsh Revival actually died because it allowed faith in the Lord's leadership to become infected with an unhealthy fear of organization and fear of human intervention. Likewise, many ministries that are built on brilliant organization often become too rigid and inflexible to hold new wine. Those who reject sound biblical leadership and organization usually become so thin that they cannot hold any wine, and it is spilled.

SEEK THE WINE, NOT JUST THE WINESKIN

Those who have tried to duplicate the original glory of the Salvation Army have, for the most part, failed. Those who have tried to duplicate the Welsh and Azusa Revivals have often become pitiful caricatures of the original revivalists. There does not seem to be a single example in church history where a wineskin of church organization was built before the new wine of revival was given. This does not necessarily mean that it cannot be done—just that it has not yet been done, and does seem to be most improbable.

Those who have tried to build the wineskin first have usually found themselves out of step and unable to receive the new wine when it came. The Lord has never restricted Himself to move by any predetermined formula. There is one quality common to those who have been mightily used by the Holy Spirit—they were able to hear the sound of the Holy Spirit moving and were willing to move the way that He wanted to for that time and place.

This is a study of two of the most remarkable moves of God of all time, but there are many others, most of which are very different, and also have much to teach us about the Lord's ways. In some way, the final move of God of this age, the greatest of all, will be a combination of them all. Though I have tried to study every true move of God that I have come across in history, to at least some degree, my greatest interest is in the one that is yet to come. It just could be that you will be one of the main characters for that one. However, many of the main characters, in that which is eternal, do not make the history books of this temporary age—but they are prominent in God's history book—the Book of Life. That is why the Lord Jesus told His disciples not to rejoice in the fact that the demons are subject to them, but rejoice to be included in the Book of Life (see Luke 10:20). That is the history book that we should all live to be included in, and it is the true source of rejoicing for those who really see.